QUESTIONS AND ANSWERS ABOUT FAITH

BY

M. FETHULLAH GÜLEN

VOL. 1

Copyright © 2000 by The Fountain

Published by The Fountain

9900 Main St. #504

Fairfax, Virginia 22031 USA

www.fountainlink.com

Translated by M. Selcuk

Library of Congress Cataloging-in-Publication Data

Gülen, M. Fethullah, 1938-

[Asrın getirdiği tereddütler. English.]

Questions and answers about faith / M. Fethullah Gülen.

p.   cm.

Includes index.

ISBN 0-9521497-1-0

1. Islam--Theology--Miscellanea. 2. Islam--Doctrines--Miscellanea.

I. Title

BP166. G8513 2000

297.2--dc21

00-010853

Printed and bound in Turkey

Table of Contents

Publisher's Note

Skepticism has been slowly subverting and destroying religious faith. In Europe, where this mood began and from where it was exported, Christianity could not withstand the doubts and questions of its adherents. The result was a widespread rejection and denial of God and religion. The Muslim world has not been immune to this malign influence. Especially in the early years of the modern age, a number of Muslims abandoned Islam while others killed themselves, saying that life without faith had no meaning.

Islamic civilization has been under cultural attack for the better part of a thousand years. The Muslims' minds and hearts of have been targeted; Islam's principles, values, and symbols have been misrepresented and abused. This led to a loss of Muslim economic and military power, which forced Islam to give up its jurisdiction over public life. In addition, this long process caused a severe decay in our collective consciousness, one that can be cured only with the medicine of the Qur'an and faith.

Islamic scholars have been aware of these facts. The late Omer Nasuhi Bilmen said: "Contemporary Islamic scholars should review the latest trends in philosophy that cast doubts and trouble into the minds of many, and should prepare new works of *kalam* (theology) to answer them."[1] Said Nursi said: "As criticism became popular and widespread, materialism

---

[1] *Muwazzah 'Ilm al-Kalam*, 21.

had the chance to infect and spread like a plague of the spirit, borrowing ideas and inspiration from science and knowledge. As it combined with a false sense of freedom and pride, it became even more widespread."

Some novels presented materialism as an imagined world designed to appeal to the whole imagination, not just the intellect. As a result, materialism's attendant attitudes spread faster than ever. In particular, they infected the minds of those young Muslims who did not read or reflect to any appreciable degree. Whether in small circles or large gatherings, skepticism was on the main agenda.

Wherever faith and religion were mentioned, always the same doubts and questions were raised. Some people who wished to respond could not do so. In effect, they closed their ears to the voices of skepticism. In the indignation of their own secure faith, they repressed their own doubts and questions. While they could not answer, their faith was simply so firm, the pleasure they took in worship so serious and profound, that doubt had no chance to take root. Some reacted excessively, accusing those who had doubts of heresy and refusing to consider the intention behind their questions.

Such attitudes and accusations only aggravated the situation. When those who honestly sought answers could not get them, they were disappointed and pushed ever closer to a dangerous moral vacuum. Some already were trapped in the downward spiral of rejection and denial. Determined materialists found this situation well suited to their purpose of establishing an ideological conflict between Islam and "modern" skepticism. This conflict caused many to deviate; at the least, it left deep scars.

In the past, unbelief was the result of ignorance. When people learned about the truth, they were enlightened and found peace of mind. Recently, however, those who follow unbelief, rejection, and denial consider themselves knowledgeable in all fields, based on their claim that they accept and believe something only on rational or scientific grounds. Such people believe that the only knowledge or understanding that they need is that which they can acquire on their own terms. Thus, their ability to seek the truth has been blunted, and very few acquire any real guidance.

The unbelievers sought to convert others to unbelief. But since the majority of those others were Muslim, the unbelievers could not do any real lasting damage. Nevertheless, cloaked in science and rational philosophy, the activity of unbelief continues in many forms, blowing like an unreliable wind from all directions. The quality of the believers' submission is impaired, for it is under constant threat and attack. Furthermore, the lifestyle engendered by modern skepticism has introduced unprecedented levels and types of vice and evil into Muslim societies. It is therefore common to meet people who have doubts and questions, and who are in danger of losing that which can secure their success here and in the hereafter.

The author of this book, sensitive to such questions, uses patient argument to answer some of these doubts and questions. Those who question in a sincere desire for knowledge will not hear themselves accused; rather, they will find clear and reasoned analyses of matters of the highest significance, analyses that will point their minds and hearts toward peace.

About the Author

Known by his simple and austere lifestyle, Fethullah Gülen, affectionately called Hodjaefendi, is a scholar of extraordinary proportions. This man for all seasons was born in Erzurum, eastern Turkey, in 1938. Upon graduation from a private Divinity school in Erzurum in 1958, he obtained his license and began to preach and teach about the importance of understanding and tolerance. His social reform efforts, begun during the 1960s, have made him one of Turkey's most well-known and respected public figures.

Though simple in outward appearance, he is original in thought and action. He embraces all humanity, and is deeply averse to unbelief, injustice, and deviation. His belief and feelings are profound, and his ideas and approach to problems are both wise and rational. A living model of love, ardor, and feeling, he is extraordinarily balanced in his thoughts, acts, and treatment of matters.

> Whenever I see a leaf fall from its branch in autumn,
> I feel as much pain as if my arm had been amputated.

Turkish intellectuals and scholars acknowledge, either tacitly or explicitly, that he is one of the most serious and important thinkers and writers, and among the wisest activists of twentieth-century Turkey or even of the Muslim world. But such accolades of his leadership of a new Islamic intellectual, social, and spiritual revival—a revival with the potential to embrace great areas of the world—do not deter him from striving to be no more than a humble servant of God and a friend to all. Desire for fame is the same as show and ostentation, a "poisonous honey" that extinguishes the heart's spiritual liveliness, is one of the golden rules he follows.

Gülen has spent his adult life voicing the cries and laments, as well as the beliefs and aspirations, of Muslims in particular and of humanity in general. He bears his own sorrows, but those of others crush him. He feels each blow delivered at humanity to be delivered first at his own heart. He feels himself so deeply and inwardly connected to creation that once he said: "Whenever I see a leaf fall from its branch in autumn, I feel as much pain as if my arm had been amputated."

Fethullah Gülen and His Mission

Gülen was born in Korucuk, Turkey, in 1938. After completing his education, he taught in Edirne and was active in religious and social services. He performed his military service, taught for some time in Edirne, and then was transferred to Izmir. This event proved to be a turning point, for it was during this time that his total dedication to religious life and interest in the general human condition became apparent. While in Izmir, he traveled from city to city to speak on subjects ranging from Darwinism to social justice in Islam, and to visit places where people gathered in order to convey his message to them.

> Applaud the good for their goodness; appreciate those
> who have believing hearts; be kind to the believers.
> Approach unbelievers so gently that
> their envy and hatred melt away.
> Like a Messiah, revive people with your breath.

Gülen dreamed of a generation that would combine intellectual "enlightenment" with pure spirituality, wisdom, and continuous activism. Being extraordinarily knowledgeable in

religious and social sciences and familiar with the principles
of "material" sciences, he instructed his students in most of
them. The first students who attended his courses in Izmir
became the vanguard of a revived generation willing to serve
his ideals.

The small group that started to form around his opinions
served people in the light of his advice. Now, many people
from all walks of life and different opinions participate in this
service. They continue to serve without thought of material
reward. They preach, teach, and establish private educational
institutions all over the world. They also publish books and
magazines, as well as dailies and weeklies, participate in television and radio broadcasts, and fund scholarships for poor
students. The companies and foundations set up by people of
different worldviews who agree on serving people, especially
in the field of education, have founded and are operating about
300 high schools and universities from England to Australia,
the United States and Russia, and in South Africa.

Only those who overflow with love
will build the happy and enlightened
world of the future.
Their lips smiling with love,
their hearts brimming with love,
their eyes radiating love and the
most tender human feelings
— such are the heroes of love who
always receive messages of love
from the rising and setting of the sun
and from the flickering light of the stars.

Further remarks

Gülen is well-known for his ardent endeavor to strength-
en bonds among people. He maintains that there are more
bonds bringing people together than those separating them.
Based on this belief, he works tirelessly for a sincere, strong

dialogue and tolerance. He was a founder of the Journalists' and Writers' Foundation, a group that promotes dialogue and tolerance among all social strata and has received a warm welcome from almost all walks of life. He regularly visits and receives leading Turkish and international figures: the Vatican's Ambassador to Turkey, the Patriarch of the Turkish Orthodox community, the Patriarch of the Turkish Armenian community, the Chief Rabbi of the Turkish Jewish community, as well as leading journalists, columnists, television and movie stars, and thinkers of varying views.

Fethullah Gülen asserts that if you wish to control masses, simply starve them for knowledge. They can escape such tyranny only through education. He believes that the road to social justice is paved with adequate, universal education, for only this will give people sufficient understanding and tolerance to respect the rights of others. To this end, he has encouraged society's elite, community leaders, industrialists, and business leaders to support quality education for the needy.

> Be so tolerant that your chest becomes
> wide like the ocean.
> Become inspired with faith and love of human beings.
> Let there be no troubled souls to whom
> you do not offer a hand and about whom
> you remain unconcerned.

His tireless efforts have begun to bear fruit, as graduates from private schools in Turkey and Central Asia, established by private donations and run as trusts, have taken top honors in university placement tests and consistently finished at the top in International Knowledge Olympics. They have produced several world champions, especially in mathematics, physics, chemistry, and biology. In fact, as recently as July 1997, a chemistry team from Izmir's Yamanlar High School took the top honors in the Chemistry Olympiad held in Calgary, Canada.

> A person is truly human if he or she learns,
> and teaches, and inspires others.
> It is difficult to regard
> as truly human someone who is ignorant and has
> no desire to learn. It is also questionable
> whether a learned person who does not renew
> and reform himself or herself to set an example
> for others is truly human.

Gülen maintains: "If a nation expects to be ignorant and free, in a state of civilization, it expects what never was and will never be." He has inspired the use of mass media, notably television, to inform those without a formal education of pressing social matters.

"As a political and governing system, democracy is the only alternative left in the world," he maintains. In spite of its many shortcomings, he states that no one has yet designed a better governing system. We must make it work. People shall always demand freedom of choice in their affairs, especially in their expression of spiritual and religious values.

> There is a mutually supportive and perfective relation
> between an individual's actions and inner life.
> We may call it a "virtuous circle." Attitudes like
> determination, perseverance, and resolve illuminate
> such a person's inner conscience;
> the brightness of one's
> inner conscience strengthens one's willpower,
> and one's resolve stimulates one to higher horizons.

"Do not despair in the face of adversity, and do not yield to those without direction," he emphasizes, lest we give up hope. He views hopelessness as a quicksand that buries human progress and kills the will to succeed, a noose that chokes and drowns people.

With his acute perception, Gülen perceives that the world's spiritual climate is undergoing a positive change. He envisions a twenty-first century in which we shall witness the sprouting of a spiritual dynamic that will revive the now-dormant moral values. He envisions an age of tolerance and understanding that will lead to cooperation among civilizations and their ultimate fusion into one body. The human spirit shall triumph in the form of an intercivilizational dialogue and a sharing of values.

Gülen successfully bridges the past with his image of the future. His deep desire to find solutions for contemporary social problems has resulted in gem-like sentences set one after another in his writings and speeches, like priceless pearls on a string. In his inimitable style and choice of vocabulary, he offers a way out of the "material quicksand" in which humanity finds itself today:

A soul without love cannot be elevated
to the horizon of human perfection.
Even if such a person lived hundreds of years,
he or she could make no advances
on the path of perfection.
Those who are deprived of love,
entangled in the nets of selfishness,
are unable to love anybody else,
and die unaware of the love deeply implanted
in the very being of existence.

"Today's men and women are searching for their Creator and the purpose of their creation," Gülen contends. He gives practical, convincing answers to such questions as: Why was I born? What is the purpose of my living? What is the meaning of death, and what does it demand from me? In his speeches and writings, one encounters statements like: "Humanity has come to a crossroads: one leads to despair, the other to salvation. May God give us the wisdom to make the right choice." His works represent a search for the truth.

He does not believe that there are any material shortages in the world, and sees no justification for starvation. Inequitably distributed wealth should be channeled through private charities to the needy. He has spearheaded the establishment of many charitable organizations to do just that.

A unique social reformer, Gülen has synthesized the positive sciences with divinity, reconciling all "apparent" differences between the two. In his writings and oral presentations, he brings the ideologies and philosophies of our part of the world and those of the West closer together.

> Compassion is the beginning of being; without it
> everything is chaos. Everything has come into
> existence through compassion, and by compassion
> it continues to exist in harmony. The Earth was put
> in order by messages coming from the other
> side of the heavens. Everything from the macrocosm
> to the microcosm has achieved an extraordinary
> harmony thanks to compassion.

"As for getting others to accept your ways," Fethullah Gülen tells us, "the days of getting things done by brute force are over. In today's enlightened world, the only way to get others to accept your ideas is by persuasion and convincing arguments. Those who resort to brute force to reach their goal are intellectually bankrupt."

In their daily lives, people must maintain the delicate balance between material and spiritual values if they are to enjoy serenity and true happiness. Unbridled greed must be guarded against.

As a student of hadith (traditions concerning the Prophet's life), *tafsir* (Qur'anic commentary), and *fiqh* (Islamic jurisprudence), as well as Sufism and philosophy, Gülen occupies his rightful place among his contemporaries in the Islamic sciences.

Currently, he is involved in organizing meetings and conferences to prepare the ground for a better century.

> Love is the most essential element in every being,
> a most radiant light and a great power
> that can resist and overcome every force.
> Love elevates every soul that absorbs it,
> and prepares it for the journey to eternity.
> Souls that have made contact with
> eternity through love exert themselves
> to implant in all other souls what they
> receive from eternity. They dedicate their
> lives to this sacred duty, for the sake of which
> they endure every kind of hardship to the end.
> Just as they pronounce "love" with
> their last breath, they also breathe love
> while being raised on the Day of Judgment.

His Works

Throughout his life, Fethullah Gülen has tasted almost nothing of worldly pleasure. He has spent his bachelor life studying, teaching, travelling, writing, and speaking. Always he feels the sufferings of people coming from the spiritual wasteland of the twentieth century.

In addition to his books, Gülen contributes to several journals and magazines. He writes the editorial page for *Sizinti*, *Yeni Ümit*, *Yagmur*, and *The Fountain* magazines. His sermons and discourses have been recorded on thousands of tapes and video cassettes. In addition, many books have been compiled from his articles, sermons, and answers to questions he has been asked over the years. Some of his books are as follows:

- *Asrın Getirdiği Tereddütler* (4 volumes; vol. 1 has appeared as Questions and Answers about Faith)

- *Kalbin Zümrüt Tepeleri* (translated as : Key Concepts in the Practice of Sufism)

- *Çağ ve Nesil* (This Era and the Young Generation)

- *Ölçü veya Yoldaki Işıklar* (4 volumes; vol. 1 has appeared as Pearls of Wisdom)

- *Zamanın Altın Dilimi* (The Golden Part of Time)

- *Renkler Kuşağında Hakikat Tomurcukları* (2 volumes; vol. 1 has appeared as Truth through Colors)

- *Kırık Mızrap* (Broken Plectrum), a collection of verse

- *Fatiha Üzerine Mülahazalar* (The Interpretation of Surat al-Fatiha)

- *Sonsuz Nur* (2 volumes, translated as Prophet Muhammad: Aspects of His Life)

- *Yitirilmiş Cennet'e Doğru* (translated as Towards the Lost Paradise)

- *İnancın Gölgesinde* (translated as:The Essentials of Islamic Faith)

Some of Hodjaefendi's books, such as *Kırık Mızrap*, *İnancın Gölgesinde*, *Sonsuz Nur*, and *Asrın Getirdiği Tereddütler* have been translated into German, Russian, Albanian, and Bulgarian.

CHAPTER 1

God

Does God Exist?

The existence of God is too evident to need any arguments. Some saintly scholars have stated that God Himself is more manifest than any other being, but those who lack insight cannot see Him. Others have said that He is concealed from direct perception because of His Self-manifestation's intensity.

However, the great influence of positivism and materialism on science humanity makes it necessary to discuss such arguments. This way of thinking reduces existence to what can be directly perceived and thereby blinds itself to the invisible dimensions of existence, which are far more vast than the visible. Since we must strive to remove the veil drawn by materialism and positivism, we will review briefly some of the traditional demonstrations for God's necessary existence.

Before doing so, it is worth reflecting upon the historical fact that, since the very beginning of human life, the overwhelming majority of humanity has believed in God's existence. This alone is enough to establish God's existence. Unbelievers cannot claim intellectual superiority over believers, for the latter contain many innovative scientists, scholars, researchers and, most importantly, saints and Prophets (the experts in this field). Also, people usually confuse the non-acceptance of something's existence with the acceptance of its non-existence. While the former is only a negation or a rejection, the latter is a judgment needing proof. No one has ever proven, and cannot prove, God's non-existence. In contrast, countless arguments prove His existence.

This point may be clarified through the following analogy: Imagine a large palace with 1,000 entrances, 999 of which are open and one of which appears to be closed. How can you claim that the palace cannot be entered? This is what unbelievers do by confining their (and others') attention only to the door which appears to be closed. The doors to God's existence are open to everybody, provided that they sincerely intend to enter through them.

Some of those doors—the demonstrations for God's existence—are as follows:

- *Creation is contingent.* In other words, it is equally possible for something to exist or not to exist. Also, it is possible for something to come into existence at any time, place, and form, and with any character. No thing or person has any role in determining how, when, or where it comes into existence, or what character and features it will have. Some power has to choose. This power must be infinite, and have absolute will and all-comprehensive knowledge. Necessarily, this power is God.

- *Things are finite.* Everything is changeable. Given this, everything is contained by time and space and therefore must have a beginning and an end. That which has a beginning needs a beginningless one to bring it into existence. As an unending regress through the originator of each originator is unacceptable, reason demands the existence of one who is infinitely self-existent and self-subsistent, who does not change. This one is God.

- *Life.* Life is a riddle but transparent. It is a riddle that scientists cannot explain with material causes, and transparent because it shows or reflects a creative power. Through both of these characteristics, life declares: "God created me."

- *Orderliness in creation.* Everything in the universe, and the universe as a whole, displays a magnificent harmony and order. This is seen in every item and in their harmonious interrelationships. This is true to such an extent that one part's existence necessitates the whole's existence, just as the whole's existence requires all its parts' existence. A single deformed cell may lead to the whole body's death. Similarly a single pomegranate requires for its existence the collaborative and cooperative existence of air, water, soil, and the sun, as well as their well-balanced mutual cooperation. Such harmony and cooperativeness point to a creator of order, one who knows everything in all its relations and characteristics, one who can put everything in order. The creator of that order is God.

- *Artistry in creation.* All creation exhibits an overwhelming artistry of dazzling worth. Yet it is created, as we see it, easily and quickly. Furthermore, creation is divided into countless families, genera, species, and even smaller groups, each of which has so many members. Despite this variety and abundance, we see only orderliness, art, and ease. This shows the existence of one with an absolute power and knowledge: God.

- *Finality in creation.* Nothing in the universe is pointless. As ecology shows in particular, everything in creation, no matter how apparently insignificant, has a significant role in existence and serves a certain purpose. The chain of creation up to humanity, the last link in creation, is evidently directed toward a final purpose. Since this requires a wise one who pursues certain purposes in creation, and since only humanity has the consciousness to pursue those purposes, the wisdom and purposiveness in creation necessarily point to God.

• *Mercy and providence.* All living and non-living beings are in continuous need of many things, even a small portion of which they cannot supply by themselves. For example, the universe's operation and maintenance demand the existence of such universal laws as growth, reproduction, gravitation, and repulsion. However, these "natural" laws have no external, visible, or material existence; their existence is completely nominal. How can something that exists only nominally, which has no knowledge and consciousness, be responsible for a miraculous creation requiring absolute knowledge and wisdom? How can it have the power of choice and preference? So, one who has all these attributes has established these natural laws and uses them to veil His operations for a certain purpose.

Plants require air, water, heat, and light. But they can obtain none of these on their own. Our needs are infinite. Fortunately, all of our essential needs, from the very beginning of our earthly existence to our death, are met by someone beyond our own capacity and intervention. We enter this world and find everything prepared to meet our all sense, intellectual, and spiritual needs. This clearly shows that one who is infinitely merciful and knowledgeable provides for all created beings in the most extraordinary way, and causes all things to collaborate to that end.

• Mutual helping. As mentioned above, everything in the universe helps everything else. This mutual helping is so comprehensive that, for example, just as almost all things (including air, water, fire, soil, the sun and sky) help us in the most extraordinarily prearranged manner, so do bodily cells, members, and systems cooperate to keep us alive. Soil, air, water, heat, and bacteria cooperate to keep plants alive. This cooperation and mutual helping, observed among unconscious beings but requiring knowledge and deliberate purpose, show the existence of one who arranges them in that miraculous way.

- *Cleanliness.* Until we began overpolluting our air, water, and land, the natural world was cleansed and purified continually. Even now, it preserves its original purity in many regions where the ways of modern civilization have not yet taken hold. Have you ever wondered why nature is so clean, why forests are so clean although many animals die there every day? Have you ever considered that if all flies born in a single summer were to survive, our planet would be covered with layers of fly bodies? Have you ever noticed that nothing is wasted in nature? Every death is the beginning of a new birth. For example, a dead body decomposes and is integrated into the ground. Elements die and are revived in plants; plants die in animal and human stomachs and are promoted to the higher rank of life.

This cycle of death and revival is one reason for the universe's continual cleanliness and purity. As well as bacteria and insects, winds and rain, black holes, and oxygen all serve to sustain the universe's purity. This purity points to one who is all-holy, whose attributes include cleanliness and purity.

- *Countenances.* Countless human beings have lived since Adam's creation. Despite their common origin—a sperm and ovum, which are formed from the same sort of foods consumed by one's parents—and although they are composed of the same structures, elements, organisms, every person has a unique countenance. This shows one with an absolutely free choice and all-encompassing knowledge, and He is God.

- *Divine teaching and directing.* To direct our lives and learn what is good or bad for us takes at least 15 years. However, many animals acquire this knowledge soon after their birth. A duckling can swim as soon as it hatches. Ants start to dig nests in the ground when they leave their cocoons. Bees and spiders quickly learn how to make their honeycombs and webs, respectively, that are such marvels that we cannot produce them. Who teaches young eels born in the Atlantic Ocean to find their way to their ancestral home in the Pacific Ocean? The birds' migration is still a mystery. How can you explain such astounding facts other than by attributing them to the teaching or directing of one who knows everything and has arranged the universe and its inhabitants in such a way that they can direct their lives?

- *The spirit and the conscience.* Despite enormous scientific advances, we cannot explain life. Life is the gift of the Ever-Living One, Who "breathes" a spirit into each embryo. Our ignorance of the spirit's nature and its relation with the body does not negate its existence. The spirit is sent to the world to be perfected and acquire a state appropriate for the other life. Our conscience is the center of our inclinations toward right and wrong. Everybody feels this conscience on some occasions. So, the spirit and conscience are strong arguments for the existence of One God.

- *Our innate dispositions and history.* We are innately disposed to good and beauty, and adverse to evil and ugliness. We also are inclined to virtues and moral values. Unless corrupted by external factors and conditions, we seek the good and moral values, which are universal. These values are the same virtues and morality promulgated by all Divine inspired religions. As history witnesses, humanity has never lived without a religion. Just as no system has superseded religion in human life, the Prophets and religious people always have been most influential people and left indelible marks on human history. This is another irrefutable proof for the existence of the One God.

- *Human intuition.* We feel many intuitions and emotions, which are a sort of message from immaterial realms. Among them, the intuition of eternity arouses in us a desire for eternity, which we seek to fulfill in many ways. However, it can be realized only through belief in and worship of the Eternal One Who inspired this intuition and desire in us. True human happiness lies in satisfying this desire for eternity.

- *Consensus.* If a few people who never tell the truth come and tell us at various times the same thing, we may believe them in the absence of any alternative. But when thousands of Prophets who never lied, and countless saints and believers who adopted truthfulness as a most essential pillar of belief, all agree that God exists, how can we reject their testimony for that of a few liars?

- *The Qur'an and other Scriptures.* Proofs for the Qur'an's Divine origin are also proofs for God's existence.[2] The

---

[2] On the Qur'an's Divine authorship, consult our article in *Questions This Modern Age Puts to Islam*, 1 (London: Truestar, 1995).

Qur'an teaches with great emphasis and force, as does the Bible in its uncorrupted parts, the existence of One God.

- *The Prophets.* Thousands of Prophets came and guided humanity to truth. All of them were justly renowned for their truthfulness and other praiseworthy virtues. All gave priority to preaching the existence and Oneness of God.

Who created God?

People with no inner spiritual life sometimes ask: If God created everything, who created God? The Prophet said that some people would ask this very question: "A day will certainly come when some people will sit with their legs crossed and ask: 'If God created everything, who created God?'"[3]

At best, the question is based on perceived "cause and effect" relationships. Everything can be thought of as an effect and attributed to a prior cause that, in turn, is attributed to a prior cause, and so on. However, we must remember that cause is only a hypothesis, for it has no objective existence. All that objectively exists is a particular sequence of circumstances that is often (but not always) repeated. If such a hypothesis is applied to existence, we cannot find a creator of the first cause, because each creator must have had a prior creator. The end result is a never-ending chain of creators.[4]

The Creator must be Self-Subsistent and One, without like or equal. If any created being "causes" anything, that capacity was created within that being, for only the Creator is Self-Existent and Self-Subsistent. Only the Creator truly creates

---

[3] Bukhari, *I'tisam*, 3.

[4] The futile notion of a never-ending chain of creators was one of the arguments used by Muslim theologians to explain the necessity of believing in God.

and determines possible causes and effects for His creation. Therefore, we speak of God as the Sustainer, who holds and gives life to all of His Creation. All causes begin in Him, and all effects end in Him. In truth, created things are "0"s that will never add up to anything, unless God bestows real value or existence by placing a positive "1" before the "0".

In the sphere of existence, what we call causes and effects have no direct or independent influence. We may have to use such words to understand how a part of creation is made intelligible to us and available for our use. But even this confirms our dependence upon God and our answerability before Him. God does not need causes and effects to create; rather, we need them to understand what He has created.

Why can't we see God?

God is absolutely other than His creation, for the Creator cannot have the same kind of being as His creation. Although this is self-evident, some people still ask why we cannot see God directly.

Direct vision is very limited. Consider the following: A tooth contains innumerable bacteria. No bacteria is aware of the tooth in which it lives, for that would mean that it has removed itself from the tooth and used some artificial means (e.g., telescopes and microscopes) to obtain an approximate idea of the tooth's surroundings and its relationship to the human body. Even if this were possible, such awareness does not mean understanding.

Our senses are in a similar situation. We know a great deal about our environment, but all of our knowledge is just a minute fragment of the whole. However, our knowledge is conditioned by understanding. We need to have a general idea about what we see in order to understand it. For exam-

ple, how could we make sense of a tree without some prior
idea, no matter how vague, of it? Given such limitations, how
can we know or see the Creator of everything?

As created and finite beings, our potential and capacity are
limited. Our Creator, on the other hand, is Infinite. We live and
die within His creation, strive for understanding and virtue,
and seek our salvation by His Mercy. Prophet Muhammad[5]
said: "Compared with the Seat of Honor, the whole universe
is as small as a ring thrown upon a desert. Similarly, compared
with the Throne, the Seat of Honor is as small as a ring thrown
upon the desert."[6] These statements show just how far His
Infinitude exceeds our power of apprehending it. If we cannot
conceive of the reality of the Seat of Honor and the Throne,
how can we even begin to conceive of Him?

In the Qur'an, we read that: *Vision comprehends Him not,
but He comprehends all vision* (6:103). After the Prophet's
ascent to the heavens, his Companions asked him if he had
seen God.[7] Abu Dharr reported that one time he answered:
"What I saw was the Light. How could I see Him?"[8] On

---

[5] In traditional Islamic literature, every mention of the Prophet is followed
by a phrase of blessing, usually "upon him be peace and blessings." In the
case of the Companions and other pious Muslims, the phrase "may God
be pleased with him (or her)" is used. Both of these are religious obligations. We have not followed this practice in this book, as it is foreign to
American literary style. This is not meant as a sign of disrespect, for they
are assumed to be there.

[6] Tabari, *Tafsir,* 3:77.

[7] The Companions of the Prophet are those who gathered around him to
receive instruction and follow his example as closely as possible. They
are considered the elite and vanguard of the Muslim nation, and are
accorded the highest respect and admiration.

[8] Muslim, *Iman,* 291; Ibn Hanbal, *Musnad,* 5:147.

another occasion he answered: "I saw a Light." [9] These statements clarify the well-known saying: "The light is the limit or
veil of God." [10] This light, which He created, stands between
us and God. We can only see by within that light, which
makes limited sight possible, and also shields or veils us from
God. Just as we see only a part of it, we also see only a part of
what veils Him.

Consider the matter from another angle. Ibrahim Haqqi
says: "In all of creation, there is nothing like, equal, or contrary to God. God is above all form. Indeed, He is immune to
and free of form." We can distinguish different things only
because they have a like, an equal, or a contrary thing. For
example, we know "long" by comparing it to "short." In the
absence of such means of comparison, as in the case of God,
we have no way to compare or distinguish. This is the meaning of "God is above all form."

Those who ask to see God directly seek to think of or
know His Being directly. Just as we cannot see Him, we cannot think of or know His Being, for He is beyond all form,
quality, quantity, and human conception or reasoning. In the
words of Muslim theologians: "Whatever conception of God
we form in our minds, He is other than it." And the Sufis say:
"God is beyond all our conceptions, and we are surrounded
by thousands of veils."

People of wisdom have said that God exists but cannot be
comprehended by human reason or perceived by human
senses. The only way to acquire knowledge of Him is via the
Prophets, whom He appointed as bearers of His Revelation.

---

[9] Muslim, *Iman,* 292.

[10] Muslim, *Iman,* 293; Ibn Maja, *Muqaddima,* 13; Ibn Hanbal, *Musnad,*
4:13.

Given this, we must accept the guidance of Revelation if we want to know about Him.

Consider the following analogy. Imagine that you are in a closed room. When someone knocks on the door, you might be able to form some vague impressions about who is knocking. However, you can only guess at his or her attributes. All that you know for certain is that someone is knocking. You can open the door and ask the person knocking to make himself or herself known to you. In this way, you can acquire more accurate knowledge of his or her true attributes.

This analogy helps us approach the question of how to seek God. Look at creation. Its sheer immensity, unity of form, beauty and harmony, usefulness and demands upon our labor and understanding make us aware of the Creator's existence. When we see a wide range of diverse fabrics produced from a single material, we know that someone has produced it, for we understand that it could not have produced itself. Similarly, we can deduce from what we can see of this creation that someone—the Creator—has made it.

But this is where the similarity ends. While we can find those who made the fabric and persuade them to make themselves known to us, we cannot do so with the Creator. This would be like the pieces of fabric demanding that their producers reveal themselves. Clearly, such a thing is impossible. Without assistance from the Creator, all we can do is speculate about who is knocking.

Revelation opens this door for us. God's Revelation to the Prophets and their teaching enable us to respond to creation as signs manifesting the Creator's Existence and Attributes.[11]

---

[11] For example, the One, the All-Merciful, the All-Compassionate, the All-Knowing, and the All-Powerful.

Through the Prophets, we learn to contemplate and call upon His Attributes. A true understanding of them requires that we follow the way of the Prophets: inner experience and contemplation, which can be achieved only by our sincere and total observance of the Divine decrees, objective study, and profound meditation. If our inner faculties are not developed, we cannot grasp the meaning of creation and so cannot contemplate the Divine Attributes manifested within creation.

Even then, not just anyone can comprehend the Divine Essence. That is why it is said: "His Names are known, His Attributes are comprehended, and His Essence exists." In the words of Abu Bakr: "To comprehend His Essence means to confess that His Essence cannot be comprehended."

Our duty is to remain committed to our covenant with God, and to beseech Him as follows:

> O You alone who are worshipped. We cannot attain to true knowledge of You, yet we believe that You are nearer to us than our jugular veins. We feel Your existence and nearness in the depths of our hearts through the universe, which You created and opened to us like a book, and through the wonderful harmony of form between all parts of Your creation. We come to perceive that we are integrated into the whole realm of Your theophanies, and thus our souls are rested and consoled, and our hearts find serenity.

Why did God create the universe?

When analyzing this issue, some facts must be kept in mind. While we perceive things from a human perspective, God does not. While we act out of necessity or desire, God does not. In other words, we cannot ascribe human attributes and motivations to God.

Who is distressed by the universe's creation? Who does not desire to enjoy its benefits or seek happiness? Very few people express real sorrow at being in this world. Some have killed themselves, but their numbers are very small. The overwhelming majority of people are glad to be alive, to be here, and to be human. Who complains of being cared for by his or her parents, or of being nourished by that love during childhood? Who complains of being a young person, during which time the exhilaration of life is felt in the very bones? Which mature adult complains of having a family, children, and leading a harmonious life with them? How can we hope to measure the happiness of Muslims who, even as they are cultivating the seed for the next world, are ensuring success in this world? They are discovering the keys to the gates of ultimate happiness, and so are content and feel no distress.

The universe, which has been ornamented with every sort of art, is like an endless parade or exhibition designed to attract us and make us reflect. Its extraordinary diversity and magnificent adornment, the sheer abundance and flow of events, present a certain reality to our senses and minds. This reality indicates the existence of an agent who brings it into being. Through the reality of His works and deeds we come to know the Doer, and so His Names. Through these Names, we try to know His Attributes. Through the channels and prayers opened to our hearts, we strive to know Him in Himself. This raising up of our being is inspired across a wide domain of reality—things, events, the vast realm of humanity's stewardship, as well as the relation or connection between us and the universe and the realm of God's Names and Attributes.

But why did God create all of this? Consider the following: Great sculptors can produce, from the hardest stone or wood, life-like statues that express the most delicate feelings. But we cannot know these sculptors as sculptors unless their abilities are revealed. We can come to know or deduce their abilities from the statues or the process used to produce them. Every potentiality wishes to reveal the reality hidden within itself, to demonstrate what it knows by assuming an outward form. Seeds strive to sprout, sperms strive to join the egg in the womb, and floating bubbles strive to reach ground as drops of water.

The urge to show our potentialities, and thus to be seen and known by others, is an expression of weakness or defect, as all beings and their wishes are merely shadows of the original essence. However, the Creator has no defect or weakness. Remember that no single or composite manifestation of the essence is similar to the actual essence.

All artistry in the universe informs us of God's Names. Each Name, displayed by what has been created, illuminates our way and guides us to knowledge of the Creator's Attributes. They stimulate and awaken our hearts by His signs and messages carried to our senses.

The Creator wills to introduce Himself to us clearly and thoroughly. He wills to show His Splendor through the variety and beauty of creation; His Will and Might through the universe's magnificent order and harmony; His Mercy, Compassion, and Grace through His bestowal of everything upon us, including our most secret wishes and desires. And He has many more Names and Attributes through which He wills to make Himself known.

In other words, He creates and places things in this world to manifest His Might and Will. By passing all things through the prism of the intellect and understanding of conscious beings, He arouses their wonder, admiration, and appreciation. Great artists manifest their talents through works of art; the Owner of the universe created it simply to manifest the Might and Omnipotence of His Creativity.

Since God knows what we will do, why does He send us here?

In short, we are sent here to improve our abilities and skills through the responsibilities He ordains for us. Not all people are created with the same ability and the same disposition; rather, they are like rough minerals waiting to be purified and refined.

For example, artists want to express their talents, and so are known by the resulting works of art. In the same way, creation's majesty, splendor, and artistry present and reflect His sacred Names and Attributes. To show us His art,[12] He created the universe and exhibited aspects of His mysterious, hidden treasures within it. To show us how His Names, Attributes, and Divine Art become manifest, He created the universe step by step. He grants us countless opportunities to know Him better and to acquire sound knowledge about Him. He is the absolute Creator who makes everything from one, and adds thousands of benefits to whatever He wills.

Humanity is placed in creation to be tested, purified, and prepared for eternal bliss in Paradise. In one *hadith*, Prophet Muhammad said: "Human beings are like minerals. One who is good in *jahiliyya* (pre-Islamic Arabia) is also good in Islam." [13] For example, 'Umar enjoyed dignity, glory, and honor before Islam, but acquired even more when he became

---

[12] For example, through His Attributes of Might, Power, Knowledge, Wisdom, Beauty, and Mercy.

[13] Bukhari, *Iman*, 10, *Anbiya'*, 8-14; Muslim, *Fada'il al-Sahaba*, 168, Manaqib, 25; Ibn Hanbal, *Musnad*, 3:101.

a Muslim.[14] He gained a calmer dignity, more tenderheartedness, and the grandeur of faith. Before his conversion, he might have been tough, quick-tempered, and haughty, one who thought he had everything; afterward, he was a most modest and humble person. Therefore, when we see well-mannered, dynamic, energetic, audacious, and spirited people, we hope that they will become Muslim.

Islam deals with the most precious and valuable mineral—humanity. It kneads, improves, and matures each individual so that all impurities are expelled. The Companions were 100 percent pure. Muslims gradually began to decline in purity, to such an extent that in our own time some people retain hardly any purity. As a result, we have experienced great troubles and problems.

God knows the final result of this test, as He is not bound by time. Therefore, He tests us so that we may become aware of what we really are by testing ourselves against ourselves and against others. This testing is a process to determine our value, to learn if we are iron or gold. We are tested in what we strive for and in what we do. One day, we shall enter God's presence and give account of ourselves: *But their hands will speak to us, and their feet bear witness to all that they did* (36:65).[15]

---

[14] 'Umar ibn al-Khattab, the second caliph of the Islamic state, was a man of high standing in pre-Islamic Makka. A fierce opponent of the Prophet, after his conversion he became one of the most respected Muslims, both in his own time and throughout history. He was a major asset to the young Muslim community.

[15] In the context of this verse, "hands and feet" symbolize everything that allows us to act, such as our body, faculties, and opportunities. In other verses, "eyes, ears, and skin" serve the same function.

What is the difference between *god*, *God*, and *Allah*?

The Arabic word *ilah* is the counterpart of the English word *god*. Both mean the thing or entity being worshipped. The Persian *khuda,* the Latin *deus,* and the Turkish *tanri* have similar meaning and connotations.

God, with a capital G, is not an exact equivalent of the term *Allah,* although we use it for practical reasons throughout this book. Rather, it is closer to the Islamic conception of *ilah.* In Arabic, *Allah* is the essential personal name of God and comprises all His Beautiful Names (*asma' al-husna*). When *Allah* is said, the One, the Supreme Being, the Creator, the Owner, the Sustainer, the All-Powerful, the All-Knowing, the All-Encompassing, whose Names and Attributes are manifested in creation, comes to mind. This term also refers to His absolute Oneness as well as His having no defect or partner. The word *God,* as used by non-Muslims, contains various conceptions and connotations that Muslims cannot accept.[16]

As *Allah* is a proper name peculiar to the One Supreme Being, we say la *ilaha illa Allah* (there is no god but Allah) instead of *la Allah illa Allah.* By saying *la ilaha illa Allah*, we first deny all non-deities and then affirm the One known by the name *Allah.* In other words, only *Allah* is *Allah,* and only He is worthy of worship.

---

[16] For example, the Christian concept of Jesus as God or the "son" of God. Of course, we should make an effort to understand what people mean when they use such ambiguous terms.

CHAPTER 2

Religion

The Qur'an says: *There is no compulsion in religion* **(2:256). What does this mean?**

Compulsion is contrary to the meaning and purpose of religion, which essentially is an appeal to beings endowed with free will to affirm and worship their Creator. Intention and volition are necessary bases of all actions (including formal worship), attitudes, and thoughts for which the individual is religiously accountable. Without that basis, accountability has no meaning. According to Islam, actions are not considered religiously acceptable or valid unless they are done with the appropriate intention. Compulsion also contradicts the religious–legal principle that actions are to be judged only by intentions.[17]

Islam does not allow Muslims to be coerced into fulfilling its rites and obligations, or non-Muslims to be forced into accepting Islam. Under Islamic rule, non-Muslims always are allowed full freedom of religion and worship if they agree to accept Islamic rule. This is indicated by their payment of *jizya* (capitation tax) and *kharaj* (land tax). In return, the state protects their lives, property, and religious rights.[18]

---

[17] Bukhari, *Bad'u al-Wahy*, 1; Muslim, *Imara,* 155; Abu Dawud, *Talaq,* 11.

[18] Traditionally, the *jizya* was not levied on non-Muslims who participated with Muslims in military engagements.

The Islamic way of life cannot be imposed or sustained by force, for faith is essential to it. And as we know, faith is a matter of the heart and conscience, both of which are beyond force. In the absolute sense, therefore, compulsion is impossible, for one can believe only with and from the heart.

From the time of Adam, religion has not coerced anyone into unbelief or forced anyone to stray from righteousness. However, the powers of unbelief always seek to coerce believers away from their religion and their faith. No believer has tried to coerce an unbeliever to become a Muslim, whereas unbelievers continually try to lead believers back to unbelief.

Some ask why some Qur'anic verses describe fighting and jihad as obligatory, on the grounds that this appears to sanction compulsion.

Fighting and physical jihad were commanded because, at that time, the unbelievers fought the believers in order to eradicate their religion. The command to fight enabled and established an ethos that recognizes the right of religious freedom and extends it to all. In other words, Islam understands and practices the principle of *there is no compulsion in religion*. Muslims had the confidence and self-assurance to understand that once that principle becomes part of the collective ethos, people will recognize Islam's truth and enter it of their own will. Historically, that is what happened throughout the territories under Islamic rule and, of course, far beyond.

We can look at this matter from another perspective. The command to wage war against unbelief pertains to certain circumstances. As civilizations rise, mature, decay, and fall, similar or the same circumstances will occur and recur. Tolerance and letting-be will be replaced by persecution, which calls for force to re-establish religious freedom. At other times, the attitude expressed in: *To you your religion, and to me my religion* (109:6) will be more appropriate.

The present is a period of the latter sort, one in which jihad is seen in our resolution, perseverance, forbearance, and devoted, patient preaching. And so we teach and explain. We do not engage in coercion, for there would be no benefit in our doing so. The misguidance and corruption of others is neither the target nor the focus of our efforts. We provoke, target, or offend no one. But, we try to preserve our own guidance in the face of misguidance. And in our own lives, we strive to establish the religion.

Just because a particular Qur'anic command is not applicable in present circumstances does mean that it is obsolete. Rather, it means that the command can be applied correctly or properly only in certain circumstances. We do not know when such circumstances will recur, only that they will. Meanwhile, the principle underlying the command remains relevant and applicable: religious persecution is abhorrent at all times and in all places. In the law and history of Islam, this principle has meant that under an Islamic polity, no non-Muslim can be coerced to enter the faith, and that all persons are free, both individually and communally, to live their faith.

Even non-Muslim, Western scholars, who often are hostile to Islam, acknowledge that Jews, Christians, and other non-Muslims ruled by Muslims generally enjoyed much greater economic prosperity, dignity, and prestige, and had far more freedoms than under non-Islamic rule—even that of their own co-religionists. Nor did this change significantly in the Western world until a thoroughgoing secularization diminished the importance of religious beliefs, rites, and solidarity. Intolerant states did not become legally tolerant so much as legally indifferent.

Religious tolerance is, in some sense, a sociopolitical characteristic special to Islam, one derived directly from the Muslims' understanding of and commitment to the Qur'anic principle of *there is no compulsion in religion.*

At present, Western political constitutions typically make space for individual religious freedom, as opposed to collective and communal religious freedom. The Islamic polity recognizes the relevance and importance of community to the practice and continuance of religious beliefs and traditions. That is why, in lieu of *jizya,* Muslims protected the lives and property as well as the rites and places of worship of their non-Muslim subjects. Also, non-Muslims were recognized as distinct communities with their own schools and institutions. The conditions for such a display of successful religious pluralism were a just, impartial central authority and the discipline of non-provocation. A collective ethos of tolerance cannot be sustained without that discipline. For example, neither Muslims nor non-Muslims were allowed to blaspheme or otherwise mock and undermine each other's beliefs and rites.

Such disciplines and related deterrent sanctions are not coercion and compulsion. Islam also applies Muslim-specific deterrent sanctions to maintain its social order and ethos. An analogy may clarify this point. Most states have armed forces composed of volunteers or conscripts. Both types of soldiers are governed by the same disciplines (and sanctions). There is no "conscription" into Islam, for you can enter only by repeating the *shahada.*[19] To be valid and acceptable, this declaration must be voluntary and sincere. After that, the duties and obligations of Islam apply equally to all Muslims.

---

[19] The Muslim profession of faith: "There is no god but God, and Muhammad is His Messenger." After reciting this statement, a person is considered a Muslim and a member of the Muslim community.

Of course, the system and its discipline is not external and as rigid as an army discipline is and has to be. Nevertheless it is a discipline, and breaches entail sanctions based on the seriousness of the matter. Typically, the disciplines of Islam are acquired gradually. Due to their inherent naturalness and ease and, most especially, because they are based on Divine and not human commands, they are readily internalized and welcomed in the heart.

When a sergeant shouts "Attention!" at his soldiers, they jump to a command that is always and only external—one obeys only because one must. By contrast, when the leader of a Muslim congregational prayer calls *Allahu akbar*, everyone present gives himself or herself the same command—it is internal as well as external. One obeys because one wants and consents to do so, and one is glad that one must. The solidarity and cohesion of a Muslim congregation (as the variety and rhythm of its members' movements demonstrates) is the solidarity of individuals gathered by consent to share in the same noble endeavor. Each fulfils his or her duty a little behind or a little ahead of another, but still together with all. It does not look like, nor is it, the mechanical solidarity of uniformed soldiers on parade.

Most breaches of discipline are slight, informal, and informally put right—usually by one Muslim advising a fellow Muslim to do the right thing and stop doing the wrong thing. Elaborating, exaggerating, or even reporting on someone's shortcomings or sins of others is considered a grave fault in Islam. Forbearance, forgiveness, patience for others, strictness for oneself—this is the more commended and generally practiced stance of the overwhelming majority of Muslims.

However, certain kinds of breaches threaten the social ethos as a whole. If such threats are not countered, the social ethos becomes eroded and society's general order and stability is undermined. Where informal private efforts to correct matters right have failed or are of no use, formal public measures, including force, must be applied. For example, Islam forbids the consumption of intoxicants, gambling, adultery, fornication, fraud, theft, and other harmful practices. It considers them both sins and crimes subject to punishment. If these vices are allowed to take root and spread, society has failed to fulfill its duty to the law and moral ethos of Islam. Collective action must be taken to prevent or undo widespread corruption within the social body. While such action includes positive efforts to educate the community in the corresponding virtues, it also must accept the negative action of imposing appropriate penalties on those who willfully and systematically introduce vices into society that will destroy its discipline and Islamic character.

Consider the issue of apostasy. Under Islamic law, apostasy is regarded with the same gravity as treason is regarded by most states and all armed forces. The hope must be to prevent, by pleading, prayers, persuasion, and all other legitimate means, such a crime from becoming public and offensive to society. Those who insist on pursuing this path must be asked to reconsider and repent. If they reject this opportunity, the penalty is death. No lesser penalty could express society's abhorrence of breaking one's covenant with God. The *shahada,* by which the individual enters Islam, is a most weighty affair. To overturn it is to insult the whole balance of creation and its relationship with the Creator. If apostasy were regarded as an individual affair only, personal conscience would be tantamount to degrading religion to a plaything, a literary toy—now a pleasure or convenience, now a displeasure or nuisance, according to the whim or caprice of the moment.

"There is no compulsion in religion" because we have free will and because "Truth stands clear of falsehood." Truth has an absolute authority within the human conscience, which calls it urgently to affirm its Creator and Sustainer. In both individual and collective life, the Truth's absolute authority demands a flexible but strong and steady discipline. Discipline and forbearance, as well as compassionate understanding and patience, are the proper responses to all breaches—but only up to and until the discipline itself is threatened with destruction. Like every discipline, the discipline of Islam imposes its burdens. But unlike any other, the rewards for carrying those burdens with sincere devotion are sanity, serenity, and ease in this life and in the life to come.

What is the point of worship, and why does it have to be done in a certain way?

Consider our position here. We are neither omnipotent nor self-sufficient, and so have needs, many of which we cannot satisfy. We are weak and vulnerable, and subject to worry, illness, and other negative events. When we look at the sheer abundance of animate and inanimate things around us, as well as their tremendous harmony and order, we cannot help but reflect on our own frailty and relative insignificance. This awakens a deeply embedded need to acknowledge the Divine, and to worship the great mysterious power that controls everything. Since whatever we can see and touch is both transient and dependent on something else, it is unworthy of our worship, for logic dictates that behind them is a Supreme Being, a Transcendent Will guiding and controlling everything. This Being, therefore, must be the goal of our worship.

Reflecting more carefully on existence, we see the all-encompassing lawfulness and order of things and events, as well as their uniformity, regularity, and obedience to an All-

Powerful Will. We thus become aware of the fact that every-thing has a part in that lawfulness and order. That part is its purpose or duty. As we realize that each one of us is also just a part, we conclude that each individual's existence cannot be a purposeless accident; rather, each individual has a specific purpose and duty to fulfil.

In aesthetic terms, we can never emulate the beauty of creation. From our own form to the vigorous and lively beau-ty of the innumerable forms and colors surrounding us, not to mention the those of the stars and planets, everything causes a strong desire within us to know the Creator. It is as if every-thing were designed and produced elsewhere and then simply placed before us so that we could marvel at them while using and benefiting from them. The world is presented as a richly laid table of foods and ornaments for our use. As we reach for any item, we inevitably sense the Giver's presence, and so experience an even greater joy and wonder.

In religious terms, such sentiments and conceptions aroused in human consciousness, as it were by nature, are a stage in acknowledging the Beautiful Names and Attributes of the Creator making Himself known through His creation. Every blessing, excellence, and beauty speaks of the one who made it possible. Every system, balance, and order indicates the one who established and sustains it. In sum, we naturally feel grateful for what God has provided and so worship Him in response to His making Himself known.

Based on this, the Mu'tazilis and (to some extent) the Maturidis,[20] say that even in the absence of Prophets or

---

[20] Two schools of thought that appeared in the early years of Islam. The Mu'tazilites used the techniques of Greek logical argument to attack orthodox Muslim theology. The Maturidis used the same techniques and argument to defend it.

guides, we should be able to gain some knowledge of God by observing the universe and then act accordingly. There is some evidence to support this argument. Before Islam, many people, including Muhammad, were born and lived in Makkah, the heartland of Arab paganism and idolatry. No one showed them the way to God or spoke to them of the Oneness of God.[21] And yet history records the remarks of a desert nomad of that time: "Camel droppings point to a camel's existence. Footprints on the sand tell of a traveler. Heaven with its stars, the Earth with its mountains and valleys, and the sea with its waves—don't they point to the All-Powerful, Knowing, Wise, and Caring Maker?"

If even a simple bedouin could understand this much, what about others? What about Muhammad, who one day would be appointed to deliver God's final Revelation? Long before the Revelation began, he understood the world's reality, perceived the Truth in the grand Book of the Universe, and began to search for it. Taking refuge in Hira cave, he devoted himself to worship. 'A'isha, narrating directly from Khadija, said that he gave himself up to prayer, only occasionally coming home for provisions.[22] This might indicate that we can reach some degree of knowledge and so worship God.

---

[21] There were no Christians or Jews in Makka. Makkans who rejected idolatry were known as Hanifs, those who had deduced by observing nature that there must be one Creator. However, they did not know anything about God or the Jewish or Christian Scriptures. The pagan Makkans, led by the Quraysh tribe, had no interest in other people's beliefs, and so sought no additional religious knowledge. Their main interests were trading, fighting other tribes, remembering their ancestors, and doing what they considered beneficial to their own interests. Already the masters of Arabia, the Quraysh felt no need or desire to learn about others.

[22] Bukhari, *Sahih,* "Bad'u al-Wahy," 3.

Zayd ibn 'Amr, 'Umar ibn al-Khattab's uncle, reached a similar understanding. Although he died before Muhammad's Prophethood, he intuitively felt the truth of Islam in the air, as well as the meaning and significance of Prophet Muhammad's coming. As he lay dying, he called his family members and said: "The light of God is on the horizon. I believe it will emerge fully very soon. I already feel its signs over our heads." Addressing God, he continued: "O Great Creator! I have not been able to know You thoroughly. Had I known, I would have put my face upon the ground before You and never raised it in quest of Your pleasure." [23]

Evidently, a pure conscience free of any traces of paganism and polytheism can understand its own station and duty via creation's splendor and harmony. Thus, it can seek to serve and please the One who created and ordained all things.

Knowing God entails worshipping Him. As he provides everything for us, we are obliged to serve Him. One of these blessings is that of prayer. God tells us how to pray so that we will do it correctly and effectively.

God told the Prophet how to pray, and we are told to follow his example. There are certain rules to follow. Before beginning, we must purify ourselves with the proper ablution. Depending on our circumstances, this can be *ghusl* (full ablution), *wudu'* (regular ablution), or *tayammum* (ablution in the absence of water). Then we say *Allahu akbar*, meaning that nothing is greater than God. Standing in a peaceful, respectful stillness, with hands joined together on our chest, indicates our complete surrender. Concentrating as fully and deeply as possible allows us to experience, based upon our level of spiritual development, the Prophet's ascension in our spirit.

---

[23] Ibn Sa'd, *Tabaqat*, 1:161-62; Ibn Hajar, *Al-Isaba*.

Rising up inwardly, we bow down physically to renew our surrender and express our humility. As we do so, we experience a different stage in our servanthood and so prostrate in fuller reverence and humility. According to the depth of surrender there, we enter into different realms. Hoping for further progress, we raise our head, say a few words, and then lower it again for the second prostration. After this, we may experience the meaning of the hadith in Muslim's *Sahih*: "The servant is never closer to God than when prostrating in worship. Make more supplications while prostrating"; and the meaning of: *Who sees you when you stand and your movements among those who prostrate themselves* (26:218-19).

Praying in the manner taught through Divine teachings and guidance is the best worship, for it flows from the love, awe, and submission to God that belief in Him and knowledge of His Divine Being engender. Following the method prescribed by God and His Prophet please Him further and benefit us the most.

We are in constant need of help, guidance, and counsel. Imagine that a successful business owner gives you sound and free advice on how to run your business. Would you refuse such advice? If we pray according to the revealed method, we avoid the pitfalls of excess and impropriety, and obtain advantage and blessings beyond our imagination. Maybe saying *Allahu akbar* releases the Divine Mercy and inspires our soul to undertake a journey like the Prophet's ascent to heaven. Maybe reciting the opening chapter of the Qur'an opens the way to the highest mystery. With every word, gesture, movement, and pattern, we may be opening hidden doors and secret locks leading to hidden realms and eternal bliss.

Prayer straightens all ways and opens all doors. God hears our recitals and supplications, and angels gather around us when we prostrate with sincerity. No one can claim that such things do *not* happen—rather, the sayings of Prophet Muhammad confirm that they do. This is why the most accepted pattern of worship is the one prescribed by God.

When we buy something, do we make up our own instructions concerning how to use it, or do we use the instructions provided by the manufacturer? As the Creator knows what will cause us to prosper in this world and the next, we should follow what He has revealed and how His Messenger practiced it in his daily life. It is we who need to worship God; not God who needs to be worshipped—He is free of all need.

What is the primordial covenant?

This matter is directly mentioned in the Qur'an:

> And whenever your Sustainer brings forth their off-spring from the loins of the children of Adam, He (thus) calls upon them to bear witness about themselves: "Am I not your Lord?"—to which they answer: "Yes, indeed, we do bear witness thereto." [Of this we remind you] lest you say on the Day of Resurrection: "Verily, we were unaware of this" (7:172).

According to this verse, every soul had to bear witness to its recognition of the Divine Existence and Unity. Qur'anic commentators continue to debate when this covenant was made. Therefore, we will look at a few considerations as to when and how and to whom this question was put.

- When we were as yet nothing and received the command *Be!*, we gave an affirmative existential response to God's creative act, which is represented or dramatized as a question–answer or a covenant.

- When were still in the form of atoms or even particles not yet formed as atoms, the Lord of the Worlds, Who cherishes and leads everything to perfection, made these particles feel the desire and joy of being human. He therefore took the promise and covenant from them, which is considered a "Yes" from all atoms to God's creative call, though it was far beyond their own power to even imagine such an affirmation.

Such question–answer or offer–acceptance is not in words or statements. For this reason, the event has been interpreted allegorically by some, as if the question were put, answered, and had a particular legal value and effect, although it is not an actual verbal or written contract. In fact, without taking into account God's power and innumerable ways of communicating with His creatures, considering this covenant to be an ordinary contract can lead only to difficulty and error.

This acknowledgement and declaration, this covenant bearing witness against ourselves as regards our recognition of the Divine Existence and Unity, is the ground of our knowing and feeling ourselves, of comprehending that we are nothing other than ourselves. In other words, this covenant is the ground of self-knowledge. It means that we start to look into the mirror of knowledge, witness the realization of diverse truths reflected in our consciousness, and acknowledge and declare that witnessing. However, the offer–acceptance, the perceiving–making perceived, the covenant, is not overt or amenable to direct perception. Perhaps it becomes perceived after many warnings and orders, and thus the significance of moral and religious guidance, counseling, and enlightenment.

The ego or self (*nafs*) is created and entrusted to us so that we may know and declare the Creator's Existence and Unity. Therefore, we prove God's Existence with our own existence, and show God's Attributes with our own attributes. For example, our deficiencies and imperfection show God's all-sufficiency and perfection; our privations show God's wealth and abundance; and our inability, weakness, and poverty show God's power, favor, and benevolence. The covenanted self is God's first favor and bestowal upon humanity. Our proper response is to know and declare God's Existence throughout creation and to perceive His Light in all lights. This is how the primordial covenant is fulfilled. The covenant is like a command that is accepted through understanding the meaning of the magnificent Book of Creation written by the Divine Power and Will, of our comprehending the secrets of the lines of events.

The question–answer of the covenant should not be thought of in a material or corporeal sense. God commands beings according to their particular individual nature, and listens to their needs and speech and whatever issues from them. Thus, He understands all and fulfils their needs. In the scholastic theologians' terminology, the Almighty understands all languages and dialects; issues commands and communicates truths in them; explains and expounds humanity and the universe; and takes promises and makes covenant with them in the form of words, for which the technical term is *kalam-i lafzi*. There is also a Divine Speech specific to animals as inspiration, and to angels as divine discourse. Although their precise natures are unknown to us, obviously it is non-verbal and consists of different manifestations of the so-called *kalam-i nafsi*.

Divine Speech is so diverse and extensive—from the inspiration coming to the human heart to the discourse addressed to the angels—and the forms of communication between the Creator and His creation are so different and occur in such different realms that those who inhabit one realm cannot hear or detect the communications belonging to another realm.

It is a serious mistake to suppose that we can hear everything. It is generally accepted that the range of our hearing, like our sight, is quite limited. What we see and hear is almost nothing when compared to that which we cannot see or hear. For this reason, God's communicating with the atoms or systems within this creation, His composing, decomposing or recomposing them, occur in such sublime ways that our limited perceptive powers cannot detect or understand them.

We cannot know exactly when God made this covenant with us, for such knowledge is beyond the ability of our limited senses and faculties. In fact, He might have made it not with our whole being, but with a specific part, such as our soul, conscience, or one of the soul's subfaculties.

There is general agreement that the human soul is an entity independent of the body. Since the soul came into existence before the physical body, and in a sense has a particular individual nature outside of time, and since the questioning and acceptance in the covenant was with the soul, our limited powers cannot comprehend or report it fully. The soul hears and speaks without words and voice, as it does in dreams, and communicates extrasensorily and without the medium of sound waves, as in telepathy.

This special form of communication is registered and recorded in its own specific way. When its time is due, it will assume its specific form and, using that language, speak and bring to the mind all original associations. At that time, we will see that the covenant has remained imprinted upon the human soul. In addition, it will be adduced as an argument against its possessor on the Day of Judgment.

All human souls were gathered in a realm that was not veiled by an intervening realm, and so saw everything clearly. After this, they swore allegiance God. When He asked them to witness against themselves: "Am I not your Lord?" they replied: "Yes, we witness that You are our Lord and our God." But some people have never turned to that section of their soul (their conscience). Thus, they have not found that profoundly inherent covenant in themselves, for they have no interest in it and have not tried to see beyond the corporeal world intervening between them and reality.

If their minds were not clouded by the conditioning biases under which they live, they would see and hear the answer to the covenant in their conscience. This is the main purpose of inward and outward, as well as subjective and objective contemplation and search. Engaging in such activities saves the mind from self-obsession and frees ideals. With an open mind and a genuinely free will, people can try to read the delicate writings in their consciences.

Some people who have habituated themselves to looking into the depths of their hearts cannot discover in books the thoughts and inspiration they acquire through such inward observation and contemplation. Even the allegorical meanings and allusive signs in the Divine Books can become manifest in their true profundity if studied in such a manner. But people cannot attain such a profound level of inward observation and contemplation, or understand what they might discover there, if they cannot overcome their own selves.

Let's look at the *when* of this covenant. It is really difficult to derive anything definite from the Qur'an and Hadith on this matter. Some commentators argue that the covenant is taken in the realm of atoms, when the person is in a state of uncomposed, separate atoms, and with the atoms and the soul of which the person will be composed. Others say that the covenant is taken while the sperm is travelling toward the egg, when the individual begins to form in the mother's womb, when it becomes a fetus, when spirit is breathed into the fetus, when the child reaches puberty, or when the person is religiously responsible for his or her actions. While each claim has its own supporting arguments, it is difficult to show a serious reason for preferring one to another.

In fact, this event could happen in the realm of spirits, in a different realm where the soul relates to or gets in touch with its own atoms, in any embryonic stage, or in any stages till the individual reaches puberty. God Almighty, Who relates to both past and present simultaneously, Who sees and hears past and present together at the same instant, could take the covenant at all of the stages mentioned. As believers, we hear such a communication from the depth of our consciences and know that our hearts have borne witness to such a covenant.

As a stomach expresses its emptiness in its own language, as a body tells its aches and pains in its own words, so the conscience informs us of this event in its own language and words. It suffers pain, distress, and affliction. Moaning with pangs of regret, it becomes restless to keep the promise made, and always hopes for the good and the best. When it draws attention by its sighs and moans, it feels relieved, fortunate and happy, just as children do when they draw their parents' attention. When it cannot express its need or find anyone to understand it, it writhes in pain and distress.

Are there any rational proofs that the covenant really took place?

Some issues that are difficult to explain by reason. Yet the possibility of such things can be mentioned. In fact, we cannot object to what God has affirmed.

Essentially, the Almighty speaks to His creations in many ways. We also use different ways and styles when communicating with others. Apart from words, we have various outer and inner faculties, sentiments and perceptions, mind and soul. Sometimes we speak to ourselves in words audible only to our hearts and minds. Such speech is not utterance, but pertains to the soul or self. At times, we communicate with others using these non-verbal methods.

At times we speak, hear, and listen to conversations in our dreams. But those who are awake and nearby hear nothing. After waking up, we tell them what we spoke and heard. So this is another mode of speech.

Some awake people can see the pictures or tablets shown to them from the World of Ideas and speak to its inhabitants. Materialists do not believe in such things, and may refer to them as hallucinations. It does not matter; let them say so... But we know that one of Prophet Muhammad's distinctions was that he was granted vision of the such tablets, pictures from the World of Ideas and from other worlds, and that he conveyed to humanity what he saw, heard, and understood. So this is another mode of speech.

Revelation to the Prophets is yet another. We know that the Prophet was fully awake and conscious when the Revelation came. Sometimes he would be lying on the ground with his head on his wife's knee, sitting and leaning against a Companion's shoulders, while his knee was touching the knee of the Companion sitting next to him, or among a group of people. At such times, he felt, received, and experienced the revelation with its full weight, and conveyed the Divine message in its entirety. Those in his presence realized, from what they could see, that the Prophet was receiving Revelation, although they could not hear it. They could "hear" and understand it only after he communicated it to them verbally. It was as if the dimensions were different.

Another way of speaking is Divine inspiration. God inspires saints, and influences, imparts, or dictates something into their hearts in such a way that they can deduce something. When they guess, or speak or act, God makes them do or say just the right thing by His mercy. So this is yet another mode of speech.

Another way of communication from heart to heart, and from mind to mind, is telepathy. This method is defined as sending thoughts or messages to another person's mind by extrasensory means. Many scientists have studied this phenomenon in the hope of benefiting from it. The atheistic and materialist Soviet regime did sustained work on telepathy, no doubt in the hope of gaining a military advantage.

Based on the above, it is clear that God created numerous, perhaps unlimited, modes of speech and communication.

Returning to the question of "Am I not your Lord?" in the primordial covenant, we do not know how God asked this question. If it took the form of Divine inspiration to saints, it would not be correct to expect some kind of audible voice. If it was a question asked of the soul, certainly it would not resemble a question asked of the body or flesh—or vice versa.

The crucial point here is that if we attempt to evaluate what they see, hear, or experience in other realms with worldly criteria and measures, we will end up in error. A *hadith* states that the angels Munkar and Nakir interrogate the dead in their graves. So, to whom or what do they direct their questions? But whether they question the soul or the body, the result is the same. Though the dead hear the questions, others

buried nearby and living passers-by cannot hear them. Even
the most sophisticated modern listening devices placed in or
near the grave will not detect anything, for it takes place in a
different dimension. Some scientists have claimed that there
are many more dimensions than just the three that are familiar to us. As place, context, and dimensions change, the mode
of interrogation and communication must change and assume
an appropriate form.

As the primordial covenant is between God and our soul,
we cannot expect to feel and retain the influence of that
instant in any physical way. Rather, we should expect it to be
reflected in our conscience, as only our conscience and the
inspirations that come to it can sense such a thing. Once,
while I was talking about this issue, someone told me that he
did not feel that *question* and *answer* of the covenant in himself. I replied: "Not feeling it is a difficulty for you. Try to
solve it."

As for me, I felt it and remember quite well that I did so.
If I am asked how I feel it, I say that it is by my desire for
eternity, and by my infinite desire despite my limited, transi-
tory existence. Essentially, I cannot know and comprehend
God because I am limited. How can I comprehend the
Unlimited, the Infinite, the Everlasting, the Absolute, the
Almighty? But because of my endless desire and enthusiasm
for the Infinite and Eternal, I realize that I feel it. I aspire to
infinity and eternity, even though I am a tiny creature in a
limited world in a limited universe; one destined to live for
a while and then die; one whose range of views and opinions
are expected to be fixed, confined, and narrow. Despite this
I yearn for Paradise, the Vision of God, and the Divine
Beauty. If I owned the whole world, my anxieties and griefs
would still torment me. Because I have such aspirations, I
say: "I felt it."

Our conscience, with all its subfaculties and sections, always tries to remain attached to God and never lies. If you give it what it requires, it can attain peace and tranquillity. That is why the Qur'an points out that our heart, which is a subtle inner faculty, can attain peace only if the conscience can attain it: *For without doubt in the remembrance of God do hearts find satisfaction* (13:28).

Such philosophers as Bergson, leaving all rational and traditional proofs aside, argue that the conscience proves God's existence. The German philosopher Kant said: "I felt the need to leave behind all the books I read in order to believe in God." Bergson refers to his "intuition," and his only proof is his conscience.

Yes, one's conscience is in agony if it rejects God, for it can find ease and satisfaction only through belief in God. If we really listen to what our conscience is saying, we will feel the desire for the Eternal and Abiding God. This feeling, perception, or quality is equivalent to the response of: "Yes, we bear witness thereto" to the question: "Am I not your Lord?" expressed silently within the human conscience. If we pay close attention, we can hear this voice, which wells up from the depths of our souls. To look for it in our mind or body is futile, for it already exists, latent and inherent, in every human conscience. However, it can prove its existence only on its own terms. Only those close to the state of the Prophets and saints, and who follow their ways, can see it clearly and make others see it.

Such matters cannot be proven in the manner of a simple, physical existent like a tree. However, those who listen to their conscience, who turn their gaze inward and observe what happens there, will see, hear, and know the primordial covenant between us and our Maker.

What does fitra (primordial nature) mean?

In an authentic hadith, Prophet Muhammad says that every new-born is born in the Islamic *fitra,* after which the parents cause the child to become either Christian or Jew or a member of another religion.

The *hadith* means that everyone has the innate potential to become a Muslim. Meaning peace, salvation and obedience, Islam is, first of all, the natural religion of all creatures. Since everything in nature has been created to render absolute obedience to God and functions according to His laws, all creatures are Muslims. Considered from the viewpoint of their bodily structure, every human being and jinn, regardless of their religion, is *muslim,* since all bodies operate according to the laws determined for them by God. If a new-born could lead a completely isolated life free of environmental effects, he or she would remain a natural Muslim.

This *hadith* has another meaning: A new-born's mind is like a blank tape on which anything can be recorded. If he or she could be protected from any external effect that would engender some impurity in his or her brain, such a person easily could receive anything related to Islam and become a perfect Muslim. But if the mind is made impure with adverse elements, or if non-Islamic dogmas and traditions are fed into it, the person will become a follower of those religions or face great difficulties while trying to become a good Muslim.

Every new-born is like a seed to grow a good Muslim, for everyone comes to the world as the seed of a future Muslim. Adverse conditions cause this seed to be deformed or spoiled and, consequently, to become a follower of another religion or, according to the surrounding conditions, of no religion at all. Therefore, improving one's family and environmental conditions is vitally important if we want to produce good

Muslims. After a child has reached the age of puberty, sins are a primary factor in deforming the seed. For this reason, it is said that every sin has the potential to guide the sinner to unbelief. So, we must do our best to protect ourselves against sins. Family, education, and environment are also of great importance for this purpose.

What is guidance? Can we guide others?

Guidance is a light kindled in someone by God as a result of his or her use of free will in the way of belief. As stated earlier, only God can guide to the truth. There are many verses in the Qur'an that state this explicitly. For example:

> If God willed, he could have brought them all to the guidance. (6:35)

> If it had been your Lord's will, all who are on the Earth would have believed, all together. (10:99)

> You do not guide whom you like, but God guides whom He wills. (28:56)

> You cannot make the dead to hear, nor can you make the deaf to hear the call when they have turned to flee. Nor can you guide the blind out of their deviation. You can make none to hear save those who believe in Our Revelation so that they surrender and become Muslims. (30:52-53)

Since it is God Who guides, we implore Him in every *rak'a* of our daily prescribed prayers: *Guide us to the Straight Path* (1:6). God's Messenger says: "I have been sent to call people to belief. It is none but God only Who guides them and places belief in their hearts."

Besides the verses above and many other similar ones, other verses state that God's Messenger calls and guides people to the Straight Path: *Surely you call them to the Straight Path* (23:73) and:

> Thus We have revealed a Spirit to you from Our
> Command. You did not know what was the Scripture,
> nor what the Faith was, but We have made it a light
> whereby We guide whom We will of Our servants.
> You are indeed guiding to the Straight Path. (42:52)

These verses are not contradictory. God creates everyone
with the potential to accept belief. However, the family, educational, and environmental conditions have a certain role in
guidance or misguidance. To call people to belief, God sent
Messengers throughout human history and gave some of them
Books whereby people could reform themselves. Prophet
Muhammad, the last Messenger, received the Qur'an from
God via revelation. The Qur'an, being the last Divine Book
and uncorrupted, contains the principles of guidance.

The Messenger's personal conduct and good example,
which embody its teaching, make his way of life a means to
guidance. He recites the Divine Revelation, shows the signs
of God, and destroys misconceptions, superstitions, and sins.
In fact, every thing, event, and phenomenon is a sign pointing to God's Existence and Unity. Therefore, if you want to
believe sincerely and without prejudice, struggle against carnal desires and the temptations of your evil-commanding
self, and use your free will to seek the truth. Then God will
guide you to one of the ways leading to Him, for He declares:

> Be aware of God and seek the means (of approach to
> and knowledge of) Him, and strive in His way in order
> that you may succeed and be prosperous [in both
> worlds]. (5:35)

> As for those who strive in Us [in Our way, for Our
> sake, and to reach Us], We guide them to Our paths;
> God is with the good. (29:69)

To find or deserve guidance, you must strive for it sincerely and search for the ways leading to it. Those whom God

has blessed with guidance should set good examples and call others to it through all lawful (Islamic) means. God commands His Messenger to do just that:

> Warn your tribe of near kindred [of their end and the consequences of their deeds and of the punishment of Hell). (26:214)

> Remind and give advice, for you are one to remind. (88:21)

> Proclaim openly and insistently what you are commanded. (15:94)

> Call to the path of your Lord with wisdom and fair exhortation, and reason with them in the most courteous manner. (16:125)

> Surely in the Messenger of God you have a good example for him who hopes for God and the Last Day, and remembers God oft. (33:21)

The Messenger communicated God's revelations and called people to belief in the best and most effective way. He bore all difficulties and persecutions, and rejected the most alluring bribes to stop calling people to belief in God. He continued his mission without expecting any worldly reward. Since he sought only God's good pleasure and people's success tin both worlds, when he conquered Makka (an event marking his triumph to make God's Word prevail among his people) he forgave those who had persecuted both him and his followers for 21 years, saying: "No reproach this day shall be on you. God will forgive you. He is the Most Merciful of the Merciful. Go! You are free."

He once told 'Ali: If someone finds guidance at your hand, this is better for you than having red camels.[24] According to

---

[24] Bukhari, *Jihad,* 102; Muslim, *Fada'il al-Sahaba*, 35.

the rule that "the one who causes is like the doer," the one who leads another to guidance receives the same reward as the new believer, without any decrease in his or her own reward. Similarly, the Messenger says:

> Whoever establishes a good path receives the same reward as those who follow that path thereafter until the Last Day, without any decrease in their reward. Whoever establishes an evil path is burdened with the same sins as those who follow it thereafter until the Last Day, without any decrease in their burden.[25]

Those who lead others to guidance should not remind them of this by saying such things as: "If I hadn't been a means to your guidance, you never would have been guided." This is a grave sin and shows ingratitude to God, for only God guides and causes one to lead another to guidance.

Similarly, those use by God to guide someone to guidance, should never attribute their deed to themselves. Rather, they should say something like: "Praise God, for He has made me, a poor and needy person, a means for so meritorious a deed as leading someone to guidance. God is so powerful, so merciful to His servants, and so munificent that He creates clusters of grapes on wood. The wood has no right to ascribe to itself the grapes growing on it. I am no better than that wood."

As for those who have found guidance, they should think: "Seeing my need and helplessness, God, my Master, used one of His servants to lead me toward guidance. All praise be to Him." Nevertheless, the one led to guidance should be thankful to the person so used by God. After all, since God is the Creator of us and whatever we do, He also creates the means

---

[25] Muslim, *Zakat*, 69; Ibn Maja, *Muqaddima*, 203.

that enable guidance and misguidance. But this does not negate or diminish our free will when it comes to guidance or misguidance.

What is the purpose of spiritual tension?

Spiritual (or *metaphysical*) tension is an inward posture, a sort of standing to moral and spiritual attention. In its positive aspect, it means that believers hold an exceptionally strong and determined disposition for all that is good and permitted. They are preoccupied with such matters, and always work to achieve them.

It has other meanings as well: a desire for religion and all things related thereto; the pursuit of religious thoughts and sentiments, ascetically and yet with love; the mind's devotion to religion, as lovers in mystical poetry constantly think of each other; preoccupation with religion at all times and in all conditions; yearning for religion to become "the life of the life," just as lovers long for union again after separation. It also means trying to awaken everybody to the thought and sense of religion, especially your own people, as the very purpose of life; being distressed and suffering for the sake of religion; establishing systems and institutions to serve people and God, and ensuring that they continue to function effectively; loving God and His Prophet more than anything else; and clasping tightly and sincerely to the way of life that the Prophet brought.

In its negative aspect, spiritual tension is being averse to unbelief, immorality, and corruption; expressing this aversion constructively; fleeing evil, vice, and destructive ways and things; and continually resisting sin and temptation.

This is how spiritual tension can preserve the vigor and vitality of believers' faith and way of life. If the believers have any weakness or are lacking in zeal, they cannot be effective servants of God, for bringing what He wills to realization is possible only through ardent desire and strenuous effort to establish the harmony, order and system that God wills. If we lack determination and perseverance, or our ourselves influenced by unbelief and misguidance and unable to free ourselves, we have lost our spiritual tension. True believers cannot step into misguidance, and our tension must be full and exact, just like our love and desire for faith.

The attitudes to be adopted and rejected so as to retain spiritual tension are defined in the Hadith. Among many others are the following: "None of you can be a believer until you love me more than you love your parents and children" and "There are three things that enable you to taste the sweetness of real belief. These are: When God and His Prophet are dearer to you than anything else, when your love for anyone is solely for God's pleasure, and turning to unbelief is as abhorrent to you as being flung into the fire."

Those who find and sense these in their conscience are aware of their belief. However deeply innate and natural filial love and relationship are, one's interest, love, relationship, and devotion to God and His Prophet ought to be stronger. We say this in the light of logic, reason, thought, and judgment. In fact, our interest in and attachment to God and His Prophet is an expression of meditation and perception, of searching and finding. Nothing else is preferable to this love, if we can reach it in our conscience by searching and meditating, and it is the first attribute of those who have tasted the sweetness of belief.

To prefer God and His Prophet to everything else means, in a broader sense, to prefer the basic elements of belief to everything else. If the love of God is in our hearts and the light of God is on our faces, everything exists and its being existent has meaning. Otherwise, there would be no difference between existence and non-existence. Believers who integrate themselves with such an understanding love all believers, and to some extent all creation, without prejudice, partiality, or ulterior motives. This is because by immersing themselves in the love of God, believers can love other persons and things only for the sake of God. This is a very important part of establishing the congregation that God wills.

It is also important to hold the spiritual tension against unbelief. Believers, if they have experienced the sweetness of belief, should feel disgust and aversion—even hatred—toward unbelief, corruption, perversion, immorality. and ingratitude. One who loses this aversion cannot desire to see unbelief eradicated from the hearts of people and replaced by belief. To realize that aim, believers must have a profound enthusiasm and love for belief and a strong hatred for unbelief. For believers' spiritual tension, and even for that of a nation and humanity, it is necessary to oppose all sorts of unbelief: evil, vice, anarchy, unrest, and disorder.

The greatest harm or enemies have inflicted upon us is to destroy our spiritual tension. They have described jihad (struggle) against unbelief as oppression and cruelty, conquest and invasion. As the poet Iqbal said, they turned lions with a glorious history into sheep. Treated in this way, those Muslims who have lost their spiritual tension remain largely unaffected by invasion, exploitation, and humiliation. Nor do they resist if their personal pride, honor, honesty or good name are attacked and blemished. Believers who maintain their spiritual tension acquire what they long for and then avoid and seek to remove what God dislikes.

In short, spiritual tension means an aversion to unbelief and error, as well as a passionate desire for belief. The crucial point here is that this tension does not mean fighting in the streets. Rather, it means living the excitement, enthusiasm, agitation, and emotions generated by the thousands of daily fights in your conscience; being in pain because of mental and spiritual suffering; being preoccupied and busy with people's problems; being ready and willing to risk all for the sake of others; "dying" and being "revived" many times a day; feeling the people's sufferings in yourself when you see them led astray, dragged toward Hell, and pulling each other down; feeling others' pangs of conscience and the tortures of Hell in your own conscience, while living in such a suffocating and lethal atmosphere of unbelief, deviation, and unawareness.

Such believers can earn the reward of martyrdom through displaying such dedication and commitment. Nothing can depress or terrorize such people—not worsening conditions, difficult circumstances, or the darkness, fog, or smoke (of ignorance)—for they are immune to unbelief. This is what we understand by spiritual tension. A society that loses this tension has perished in its spirit already, even though its outer form continues to exist. God allows oppressors and tyrants to attack such societies, to send their corpses the way of their already departed souls.

Death begins in the soul and heart, and later takes the body away. Physical defeat always follows spiritual defeat. God never lets people who keep their souls alive to be downtrodden. Those who cannot sustain their spiritual tension are destined to die. It is mere caprice and fancy for such people to suppose that they have a religious life. If a revival does take place, it is because some people have retained their spiritual tension. The only reliable support and power in all affairs is from God only.

How can spiritual tension be restored?

Maintaining spiritual tension is harder than getting it. That is why determination and perseverance are needed to get it. Tension slackens due to familiarity and habit. Believers may become used to the terms and ways of their cause, and so gradually grow bored with it. Sometimes selfishness, passion, ambition, envy, covetousness, avarice, love for rank and position, comfort, and lethargy dampen their enthusiasm and love for acting upon and serving in the way of God. Such a development can result in the loss of already acquired spiritual qualities and a paralyzed willpower. If active believers start making excuses and not showing up where they are expected, their tension is slackening and they are in danger of losing it altogether. Without spiritual tension, believers cannot serve God, Islam, and people.

Fortunately, there are people around us who should be praised for their good examples in this regard. For instance, I will never forget the reply of one such person when I asked him for some reason whether or not he had stayed at home for a couple of days: "I never stay at home after I have undertaken a task."

Doctors prescribe medications and inoculations for illnesses and advise us to follow their recommendations closely, whether we want to or not. We pay attention to and follow such medical advice for our physical disorders. Should we not be even more (or at least equally) attentive to what is prescribed for our spiritual disorders? How can we preserve our spiritual tension, and ultimately attain the companionship of the Prophet and his Companions, if we are not attentive to such matters?

I have several recommendations:

- Do not stay alone, for "the wolf will devour a lamb that has left the flock." Those who are separate from their congregation and stay away from their friends will devoured by Satan. Their decline starts by lamenting that which they could not do. While it lasts, such an activity is good. However, soon they will begin to criticize and belittle their friends' activities, an attitude that worsens little by little until they deny the purpose and ideals of the cause and starts to claim that what is being done is inappropriate or unnecessary. When this point is reached, such people are in serious danger of becoming lost. They can be rescued only if their absence from the congregation and isolation from their friends are put right. This is why all possible gateways leading to this outcome must be kept shut from the outset.

- Always look for fresh ways to extend and revive your learning and knowledge, spiritual knowledge in particular, and be persistent and consistent in seeking. God opened the universe like a book before our eyes, and sent Prophets and Divine Books to teach us about it. Countless pious saints and learned scholars have soared in knowledge and wisdom, seeking to understand and explain the book of the Laws (the Shari'a) and the book of creation. Like honeybees collecting from thousands of flowers, they contributed their part in producing wholesome honey in their hives of knowledge. Everything should be studied carefully and evaluated as happening in accordance with the requirements and purposiveness of Divine Wisdom. If we can do this, we can say that we are acting in harmony with Divine Wisdom. Those who cannot do so gradually lose their vitality in the basis of knowledge and quickly fall into decay and corruption. After a while, they become ineffectual.

- Contemplation of death is also an important factor here. Dying before one's appointed time is another name for attaining real life. To cut away the interminable worldly ambitions that exhaust us is only possible by death, by understanding that all of our true friends are waiting for us, and that true happiness and bliss exist on the other side of the grave.

Is it not our highest ideal to reach the beloved friend (the Prophet), Paradise, and the Divine Beauty? We should try our best, and never avoid any hardships in the way that leads to that point. I like horses very much and use the simile of a horse to describe people who follow the cause of God. A horse never says it is tired or offers excuses while running, and runs until its heart breaks and it dies. Death becomes its excuse for not running. All of us who strive in His cause should be like horses—we should run in the way of God, without pause or excuse, until we die.

- Choose a friend who will rouse, caution, and warn you. Such friends will notice our slackness and put us back on track by warning and counseling. Though it might be a little awkward at first, following this suggestion will result only in good.

As soon as you feel a little slackness, a deflection in your heart, and a lack of enthusiasm, talk with your friend and let him know what is going on. Your friend will help you recover. Although the advice may strike you at first as a little harsh, even offending, only good will result, for it will save you from even more painful situations and replace your spiritual pain with spiritual pleasure. I have often turned to such a friend, someone who is younger than me and used to be my student, and his suggestions always have benefited me. Everyone can form such a relationship, provided that it is done gratis and for the love of God.

- We have a proverb that says: "Working iron does not get rusty." This applies to those who serve God. It is a psychological fact that we are more concerned with our own affairs than those with others, for even if they are important in principle, they affect us only secondarily and indirectly. This natural psychological disposition should be evaluated and used carefully. Each person should assume a responsibility and a task, whether small or large, and assume ownership or sponsorship of the services done or to be done.

As long as we sincerely follow these suggestions, *in sha' Allah* we will preserve and strengthen our spiritual tension and reach the horizon of active women and men of service.

Will religion, supposedly developed by "primitive" people to explain the unknown, eventually become unnecessary?

Those who answer the above question with a resounding "yes" base their answer upon the following suppositions: People who could not explain or control a certain natural phenomenon attributed it to a creator. Or, people gave certain beneficial natural yet unreliable phenomena an aura of sacredness. In some cases, this went as far as deification. Supposedly, this was how the Ganges became sacred to the Indians, the Nile to the Egyptians, and cows to both of them. Confronted by insecurity, people sought security by revering and appeasing the supposed source of security or insecurity.

Some cultures split this aura of sacredness between two deities, one good the other evil, which led to attributing love and mercy to one, and terror and punishment to the other. The argument also is used to explain Heaven and Hell, and eventually concludes that religion became a comforting middle-class illusion and tool used by the powerful and the religious establishment to manipulate the masses. In other words, in communist terminology, religion became the opiate of the people.

I reject this argument for the following reason: Religion is not a byproduct of fear or a lack of reason.

The Arabic word for religion is *din*. Among its many meanings are obedience, recompense, and a path. These meanings are interlinked. The path is the way that leads, through obedience, to God, the All-Mighty. After we die, we will have to give a full account of what we did while on this path. In a more technical sense, *din* may be defined as "the complete Divine Law that guides a person of sound mind to do good." Just as the law distinguishes a legally responsible person from one who is not legally responsible, the demands of the religious life are addressed to people who can reason. Religion exists because we can reason and understand.

Furthermore, our free will allows us to obey or disobey God. Obedience is required, but it is not imposed. The idea that religion comes about simply because some benefit is desired in an area beyond human control is untenable. True religion does not negate free will. On the contrary, it points out that nature was created to benefit us and to enlarge our potential. It also emphasizes that we can choose our own way by exercising our God-given freedom to do so.

As for religion being an outgrowth of defective reason, I beg to differ. In truth, religion is primarily grounded in faith.[26] Although we can deduce the existence of the universe's Creator through reason, such a deduction is vulnerable and insecure. Sound belief in God is possible only through a true Prophet's guidance. Every Prophet was endowed with certain signs (e.g., miracles) confirming his appointment by God. The Divine Scripture with which he was sent is the most significant miracle. Regardless of when we were born, we are required to follow the Book and the Prophet's beliefs and actions.

A Prophet does not exercise ordinary worldly power over his followers. Rather, all Prophets endured extraordinary hardship and suffering. They demanded and expected nothing from the world, although they could have acquired whatever they desired if they agreed to abandon their missions. Prophet Muhammad experienced Heaven's beauties and spiritual delights during his miraculous ascent to the Divine Presence. Yet he chose to return to his people and endure their torment, contempt, and ridicule. He was not a man of physical or spiritual pleasure, but one who had dedicated his life to serving humanity for the sake of God.

---

[26] Islam demands rational and spiritual conviction based on thinking, reasoning, searching, and verification. People can base their initial faith on imitation, but they cannot remain at that stage if they want to be serious believers. The Qur'an contains over 700 verses urging people to study natural phenomena, to think, reason, search, observe, take lessons, reflect, and verify. Many verses conclude with such phrases as: *Will you not use your reason; will you not think; will you not reflect; will you not take lessons;* and *take lessons, O people of insight.* The Qur'an describes unbelievers as people without intellect and unable to think, reflect, see, and hear. The very first verse revealed to the Prophet was: *Read in the name of Your Lord* (96:1), a clear indication that one's faith and belief cannot be blind.

Some might ask if anyone can have direct access to God and so receive a Revelation. This is impossible, for only a person with a perfectly purified soul can receive Revelation. And, one can have a perfectly purified soul only because God chooses and then purifies him so that he can be endowed with Prophethood: *God chooses Messengers from the angels and from humanity* (22:75).[27] Just as God chose Gabriel to convey His message to His Messenger, so He chose the Prophets to teach the true religion. They were men of pure character, and their companions were distinguished souls entrusted with transmitting the religion to future generations.

If the argument that religion grows out of humanity's need to cope with difficult events or certain natural phenomena had any foundation, we would expect it to be occasional. When the need for it had passed, it should have faded away, only to re-emerge when a similar need arose. But Islam is not concerned merely with birth, death, and marriage ceremonies or with solving a personal or collective crisis. Rather, Islam concerns itself with the entire life of each individual and of each society. It guides and protects all ordinary daily affairs, even those under our control. The call to prayer comes throughout the day, every day, and is directed to everyone, regardless of class or other criterion. It is not an answer to eclipses, thunderbolts, or other natural phenomena, but the divinely revealed way for each individual to become worthy of faith and able to choose goodness.

The vigor and stability of our faith depends upon worship and good deeds. Muslims who neglect the religious obligations may end up doing little more than speaking well of certain ancestors who lived a disciplined, religious life. Faith not

---

[27] According to Islam, only men can be Prophets or Messengers. The reasons for this are given in the chapter on Prophet and Prophethood.

nourished by worship and good deeds eventually dies. Praying five times a day strengthens our faith and renews our covenant with God. As long as we worship with an alert and conscious intent, we receive assurance from God and thereby strengthen our will and ability to fulfill all our obligations.

Islam contains certain rules and norms to order our every-day life. For example, Muslims are required to seek God's approval through their dealings with others as well as through formal or informal prayer. Commercial transactions must adhere to the Divine Law, another element that reinforces faith. By doing so, Muslims submit to the God's decree in that particular matter and so transcend their own worldly preferences. For example, Muslim merchants must inform their customers of any defect in the merchandise. While this will lower or even cancel the resulting profit, Muslim mer-chants who do so will have the satisfaction of obeying God and not serving their own desires. When they pray, this satis-faction will return to strengthen their faith and commitment.

Such observance gives us a practical means to reach the Divine Presence. The Messenger told us to aspire to this end. He once related a story of three men who, trapped in a cave by a boulder, promised God that they would do a good deed if He allowed them to get out of the cave alive. While we cannot resemble the Messenger physically, we can—and should—try to resemble him in our behavior and actions. Doing so is our way of promising God that we will do good deeds if He will protect us from Hell.

Islam teaches that virtue also consists of avoiding sins.[28] Pursuing virtue, whether by observance or avoidance, prayer

---

[28] Islam defines sin as that which God has forbidden. Some of the best known are avoiding alcohol, drugs, pork, sexual relations outside the mar-riage bond, and dealing with interest.

and remembrance, or establishing the Revealed Law and justice, are essential elements of Islam's unity. Such unity is integral, for one part cannot be separated from another. Faith, worship, remembrance of God, the Prophet's example, and the Divine law are all vital and integral elements of the *din*.

God created humanity as His vicegerent on Earth. As He is Himself Absolute, Transcendent, and independent of all things, He does not need our worship. Rather, it is we who need to worship Him. We do so by His will, for we cannot manage it ourselves. God wills, as spelled out in the Qur'an, that we lead a balanced life. He has opened a clear, straight path so that we will not go astray. If we follow this straight path (the Qur'an), we can develop our full individual and collective potential and attain to true humanity.

We need religion. Indeed, if we understood what we truly need, we would realize, acknowledge, and cultivate our innate disposition toward eternal happiness. We would proclaim our true need and desire: "O God, give us a way of which You approve, so that we may be safe from any deviance."

While even the wisest philosophers have gone astray, the most ordinary Muslims have been able to lead upright lives because they followed the clear way of Prophet Muhammad. Indeed, Muslims who seek God's approval and take the Prophet as their guide can lead a most fruitful life, one in harmony with their deepest nature as responsive and responsible creatures of God.

Religion is not formulated by some people to manipulate others or to cope with the natural world. God revealed religion out of His Mercy, because we need it and cannot be truly human without it. Only those who have passed through the trials of religious experience are worthy of eternal happiness and will be distinguished in the Hereafter. The Messenger said:

"As you distinguish your horse in a herd by the blaze on its head, so will I distinguish my community in the Hereafter by the brightness of the parts of the body washed in *wudu'*." [29]

The clear way of Divine religion consists of fundamentals and branches. The fundamentals always have been the same for all Divinely revealed religions, although the branches (how to worship and observances) have differed. God placed certain methods of worship upon a people according to their prevailing social conditions and capacities.

For example, belief in the Resurrection has been central to every religion, and every Prophet preached it. If this had not been so, religion would have been reduced to a socioeconomic or psychological system of rules and norms, and thus powerless to inspire good and prevent evil. If this belief had not existed, sincere worship of God and sincere sacrifice for His sake would not have been performed. We acquire many virtues by believing *that whoever has done an atom's weight of good shall see it, and whoever has done an atom's weight of evil shall see it* (99:7-8). In trying to follow His way as closely as we can, we look forward to that moment when we shall see Him without any veil.

Alongside such constant fundamentals, God has revealed changes in His Law by abrogating what went before. This does not mean that He changed His mind. Rather, it represents His Mercy in response to our moving through a stage of infancy (the time of Prophet Adam) to one of maturity (the time of Prophet Muhammad).[30] As the last and most perfect Divine religion, Islam will prevail until the Day of Judgment.

---

[29] Bukhari, *Wudu'*, 3; Muslim, *Taharah*, 34, 35; Ibn Hanbal, *Musnad*, 2:334, 362, 400, 523.

[30] *Musannaf*, 11:428.

Even if the earlier Scriptures and Laws had retained their original purity, they could not have retained their legitimacy, since their authority from God was abrogated by the advent of Islam.

In conclusion, true religion is the assemblage of Divine Revelations and Divine Laws by which we can know bliss in this world and the next. Our peace and happiness depend upon leading a religious life, for only through religion can the Law be observed in all the inner and outer spheres of our existence. Only religion makes it possible for us to deserve Paradise and the vision of God. Such achievements are beyond the power of every human-made civilization, regardless of how advanced they are.

Submission, sense, and reason

Many people ask how Islam, which requires submission to God, can be in accord with sense and reason. What we must realize here is that these two realities are not mutually exclusive. Islam does mean submission to God, and Islam is indeed in accord with sense and reason.

The principles of Muslim life are set forth in the Qur'an. If they were not, how could we know them? The Qur'an is an uncorrupted revelation of reality. The demonstrations presented therein concerning Divinity require Prophethood, since only Prophets can make the Divine known to humanity. Such demonstrations appeal to reason and sense, as do those concerning death and resurrection. Our intuition of eternity actually arises from eternal life itself. If this were not so, how could we intuit its existence, based upon our limited human knowledge and experience?

I will limit myself to arguing that all matters related to faith in Islam can be demonstrated by reason. Yet such demonstration means little or nothing at the level of truly profound human perception.

By definition, every act of God accords with sense and reason, for He is the All-Wise and the All-Knowing. We are bound to conclude that our best works, when compared to His, are of almost no significance. This world, which He gave us to live in, always will far exceed all that our living can add to it. Moreover, we can add to it only what God allows us to add. Given this, we can deduce that each of God's actions has a definite purpose. This realization is wholly pleasing to sense and reason.

All that we see around us when contemplating the Divine laws so evident in His creation, as well as our inner personal conviction, makes it impossible for us not to believe in God. That belief in God, that sense of His Being, whether in the outer world or within ourselves, inevitably leads us to submit to Him. In this way, a path moving from sense and reason ends in submission. And submission means a willing, intended obedience to God by obeying all His commands and prohibitions.

God has sure reasons for His commands and prohibitions, some of which we can understand. One such reason is that they are for our own individual or collective benefit. Take the five daily prayers, each of which must be prayed during its allotted time. Some benefits are immediately obvious: self-discipline and order, stability of faith and community. The manner of praying also is prescribed for definite reasons. The value of washing certain bodily parts before worship has obvious health and other benefits. Congregational prayer enables and sustains the community's existence. Zakat (the alms-tax) contributes significantly to preserving responsibility and balance between rich and poor people. Fasting has undeniable health benefits. As a further example, the Islamic penal code, (when applied by God-conscious rulers and) if studied in the light of sense and reason, leads to submission to the All-Wise and All-Mighty.

Regarding pilgrimage (hajj), the Qur'an says: *Pilgrimage to the House is a duty to God for all who are able to make the journey* (3:97). Obeying this command is an act of submission that leads to the experience of hajj, which leads us to contemplate its benefits: a worldwide conference for Muslims, an occasion for us to be together for the sake of God and free of all human and therefore artificial discrimination based on race, sex, color, or level of education.

Whether we start from an act of submission and the use of our sense and reason, or use our sense and reason and then are led to submission, Islam is confirmed, for it is grounded in sense, reason, and submission.

Can Islam solve every problem?

Yes, it can. What we say on this subject has been said already by many people. The many conversions to Islam even in the West are a strong argument for Islam's ability to solve a wide range of problems.

Who knows how to run a factory better than its designer and builder? When we want to get a simple electronic device to work, we consult someone before we use it. In the same way, the One who created us knows best how our individual and social life should be conducted. Obviously, He also would give us the best and the most suitable system by which to conduct ourselves: Islam.

Today we can see the ruin of human-made systems all around us. Corrupt and bankrupt, held up for a while by temporary success, they nevertheless continue to crumble.

Feudalism, capitalism, socialism, and communism all have collapsed or are in ruins, leaving behind nothing but distress and lamentation. Islam, however, remains with us and has lost none of its original vigor. The West is well aware of this, for many of its people warmly welcome Muslim spiritual guides and preachers. Even some churches are used to serve Islam in one way or another. The world is moving toward a new understanding of Islam, and there is widespread conviction that Islam will solve our "unsolvable" problems.

If your enemies appreciate your virtues, you are indeed worthy of admiration. Today, even the enemies of Islam seem to have recognized its virtues. In Europe, many who have accepted Islam do not confess it publicly due to social or political fear. Moreover, most of them are members of the church.

To get a concrete, substantial answer, we must ask a specific, detailed question. To deal with all problems and indicate how Islam resolves each one within the confines of this book is impossible. If those who argue that Islam cannot solve our problems would indicate a particular problem, I would be happy to provide a particular answer.

Why does Islam allow slavery?

There are historical, social, and psychological dimensions to this question. First, the very word *slavery* conjures up revulsion, sorrow, and deep disgust, especially when we remember how slaves were treated in ancient Rome and Egypt. Pictures of people building the pyramids, of gladiators fighting each other to the death for the spectators' amusement, and of people bound by shameful yokes and chains around their necks come to mind when we hear that word.

Nearer to our own time, we have the western European variety of slavery. The barbarity and bestiality of this enormous trade beggars all description. The trade was principally in Africans who were transported across the oceans, packed in specially designed ships, and considered and treated as livestock. These slaves were forced to change their names, abandon their religion and language, deprived of all hope for freedom, and were kept for labor or breeding purposes. A birth among them was celebrated as if it were a death.

It is hard to understand how human beings could conceive of fellow human beings in such a light, still less treat them thus. But it happened. Documentary evidence shows how shipmasters would throw the slaves overboard to claim compensation. Slaves had no legal or other rights, but only obligations. Their owners had the absolute right to dispose of them as they wished-brothers and sisters, parents and children, were separated or allowed to stay together according to the owner's mood or economic convenience.

Centuries of this dreadful practice made western Europe rich from its slave-based exploitation of such commodities as sugar, cotton, coffee. When it abolished slavery, first as a trade and then altogether with much self-congratulation, only the slave-owners were compensated. In other words, the attitudes that made slavery possible remained.

Soon after its abolition, Africa was colonized by western Europe with consequences for the Africans no less terrible than slavery itself. Moreover, as their attitude to non-Europeans has changed little, if at all, the slaves' descendants continue to live in poor social and political conditions. Those who live amid Europeans remain despised inferiors. Museums in western European capitals only closed their public displays of bones and stuffed bodies of fellow (but non-white) human beings several decades ago—displays organized by European scientists, doctors, learned people, and humanitarians.

In short, the institution of slavery disgusts the human heart, as do the attitudes of inhumanity that sustain it. If the institution no longer formally exists but the attitudes persist, can we say that humanity has made any progress? This is why colonial exploitation replaced slavery, and why the chains of unbearable, unrepayable international debt have replaced colonial exploitation. Slavery has disappeared, but its inhuman and barbarous structures are still securely in place.

Before we turn to the Islamic perspective on slavery, let's recall a name famous even among western Europeans: Harun al-Rashid. This ruler, who enjoyed such authority and power over Muslims, was the son of a slave. Nor is he the only such example. Slaves and their children enjoyed enormous prestige, authority, respect, and (shall we say it) freedom within the Islamic system, in all cultural, political, and other spheres of life. How was this possible?

Islam amended the institution of slavery and educated masters about slaves. The Qur'an often states that everyone is descended from a single ancestor (Adam), and that no one is inherently superior to anyone else because of race, nation, or social standing. The Prophet applied these principles in his own life, and his Companions learned them and accepted them as laws and as social norms. The Prophet stated:

> Whoever kills a slave shall be killed. Whoever imprisons and starves a slave will be imprisoned and starved. Whoever castrates a slave will be castrated.[31]

> You are sons of Adam, and Adam was created from clay.[32]

---

[31] Abu Dawud, *Diyat,* 70; Tirmidhi, *Diyat,* 17; al-Nasa'i, *Qasama,* 10:16.

[32] Tirmidhi, *Tafsir,* 49; *Manaqib,* 73; Abu Dawud, *Adab,* 111.

No Arab is superior to a non-Arab, and no non-Arab is superior to an Arab. No white person is superior to a black person, and no black person is superior to a white person. Superiority is based on righteousness and God-fearing alone.[33]

Due to this compassion, slaves and those described as poor and lowly were respected by those who enjoyed high social status.[34] 'Umar expressed such respect when he said: "Master Bilal, whom Master Abu Bakr set free."[35]

Unlike other civilizations, Islam requires that slaves be thought of and treated within the framework of universal human brotherhood. The Prophet said: "Your servants and your slaves are your brothers (and sisters). Those who have slaves should give them from what they eat and wear. They should not charge their slaves with work beyond their capabilities. If you must set them to hard work, in any case I advise you to help them."[36] He also said: "None of you should (when introducing someone) say: 'This is my (male) slave' or 'This is my female slave.' Rather, call them 'my daughter,' 'my son,' or 'my brother.'"[37]

---

[33] Ibn Hanbal, *Musnad*, 411.

[34] Muslim, *Birr*, 138; *Jannat*, 48; Tirmidhi, *Manaqib*, 54, 65.

[35] Bilal, one of the earliest Muslims, was a black Ethiopian slave. He eventually was chosen by the Prophet to be the official *muezzin* (caller to prayer) of the Muslim community. Abu Bakr, one of the pre-Islamic Makkan elite and also an early convert, was the Prophet's political successor and the first of the Rightly-Guided Caliphs. Bukhari, *Fada'il al-Sahaba*, 23.

[36] Bukhari, *Iman*, 22 and *Adab*, 44; Muslim, *Iman*, 38-40; Abu Dawud, *Adab*, 124.

[37] Ibn Hanbal, *Musnad*, 2:4.

For this reason, 'Umar and his slave took turns riding a camel while traveling from Madina to Jerusalem to take control of Masjid al-Aqsa. While he was caliph, 'Uthman had his slave pull his own ears in public, since he had pulled his. The Companion Abu Dharr, applying the hadith literally, made his slave wear one half of his suit while he wore the other half. These Muslims, and many others, showed succeeding generations of Muslims how to treat slaves as full human beings worthy of the same respect, dignity, and justice given to non-slaves.

This constructive and positive treatment necessarily affected the master's attitude. Slaves retained their humanity and moral dignity, and had a place within the master's family. Even when they were freed, not all wanted to leave their masters. Starting with Zayd ibn Harith,[38] this practice became quite common. Although the Prophet gave Zayd his freedom, the latter chose to remain. Masters and slaves were able to regard each other as brothers and sisters because their faith enabled them to understand that differences between people are not permanent. Therefore, neither haughtiness nor rancor were acceptable.

In addition, there were strict principles enforced as law, such as: "Whoever kills a slave shall be killed; whoever imprisons and starves a slave shall be imprisoned and starved."[39] Besides sanctions mandating proper treatment, slaves also

---

[38] Zayd ibn Harith was a black slave who had been owned by Khadijah, a wealthy Makkan widow and merchant. Upon her marriage to Muhammad, who had not yet been given Prophethood by God, she gave him to her new husband as a gift. Muhammad adopted him as his own son and treated him as such, until God revealed years later that such a relationship was no longer allowed.

[39] Tirmidhi, *Al-Ayman wa al-Nudhur*, 13.

enjoyed the legal right to earn money and hold property independently of their masters, to keep their religion, and to have a family and family life with the attendant rights and obligations. Along with personal dignity and a degree of material security, Islamic laws and norms allowed slaves a still more precious opening—the hope and means of freedom.

Human freedom is God-given, and therefore everyone's natural and proper condition. Thus to restore a person, either wholly or partly, to this condition is one of the highest virtues. Freeing half of a slave's body is considered equal to saving half of one's own body from God's wrath in the next world. Freeing a slave's whole body is considered equal to saving one's whole body. Seeking freedom for enslaved people is an acceptable reason for engaging in warfare. Muslims were encouraged to enter into agreements and contracts that enabled slaves to earn or be granted their freedom after a certain time or, most typically, on the owner's death. Unconditional emancipation was regarded as most meritorious and worthy in the Hereafter. Sometimes groups of people would buy and free large numbers of slaves in order to obtain God's favor.

Freeing a slave also was the legal expiation for certain sins or failures in religious duties, such as breaking an oath or a fast—a good deed to cancel a moral lapse. The Qur'an orders that a person who accidentally kills a Muslim must free a believing slave and pay the blood-money to the victim's family (4:92). A killing affects both the society and the victim's family. The blood-money is a partial compensation for the latter, while freeing a slave is a bill paid to the community—it gains a free person. To free a living person in return for a death was considered like bringing someone back to life. Both personal and public wealth was used to free slaves. The Prophet and Abu Bakr were known for this practice. Later on, especially during the reign of 'Umar ibn 'Abd al-'Aziz, public zakat funds were used for this purpose.

A possible question: Islam regards slavery as a social evil, regardless of how well slaves are treated or how many rights they enjoy. Therefore, why was it not abolished, as happened with alcohol, interest, gambling, or prostitution? Why did the Prophet condone it?

Until the evil of the European slave trade, slavery was largely a byproduct of war, for the victors normally enslaved the survivors. During Islam's early years, there was no reliable system of exchanging prisoners of war. The available means of dealing with them were execution, placing them in prison, allowing them to go home, or distributing them among the Muslims as spoils of war.

The first option must be ruled out on the grounds of its barbarity. The second is practicable only for small numbers and for a limited period of time, provided that there are enough resources to care for them. This option was used, for prisoners were taken in the hope of ransom payments. Many Makkans held by the Muslims were so satisfied with their treatment that they became Muslims and changed sides. The third option is imprudent in times of war. This leaves, as a general practice, only the fourth option. Islam instituted humane laws and norms for what is, in effect, the rehabilitation of prisoners of war.

While living among Muslims, slaves saw at close quarters the truth of Islam in practice. Many slaves were won over by the kind treatment they received and Islam's humanity, not to mention their access to many of the legal rights enjoyed by Muslims, and, ultimately, by the chance to regain their freedom. Thousands of ex-slaves can be found among the great and famous names in Islam, and their won examples became a norm for future Muslims—imams such as Nafi' (Imam Malik's teacher) and Tawus ibn Qaisan, to name only two.

In general, Muslims considered slavery a temporary condition. Unlike Western civilization, whose values are now so much in fashion, slavery was not an inherited condition that engulfed whole generations in deepening spirals of degradation, despair, and hopelessness.[40] On the contrary, enjoying a status as fundamentally equal to everyone else, slaves in Muslim society could and did live in secure possession of their dignity as creatures of the same Creator. They had access to the mainstream of Islamic culture and civilization—to which, as we have noted, they contributed greatly. In Western societies where slavery was widespread, particularly in North and South America, the descendants of slaves, even generations after their ancestors' formal emancipation, remain largely on the fringes of society, a subculture or anti-culture—which is only sometimes tolerated, and mostly despised, by the dominant community.

When the Muslims were secure against foreign conquest, why did they not free all of their former captives or slaves? Again, the answer has to do with existing realities. Those former captives or slaves did not have the personal, psychological, or economic resources needed to establish a secure and

---

[40] Children born to enslaved women were considered free in Islamic societies. Under the Ottomans, palace harems served as schools that educated its members to serve as palace personnel, such as servants to the sultan's family. Some were raised to be the sultan's future wives, while others were married to palace personnel. Viziers and barons tended to marry such women to avoid any land-related problems (e.g., all land theoretically belonged to the sultan) and disputes among heirs. The *andarun*, the male counterpart of the harem, educated its members for civil administration. Both institutions were run according to very strict rules and provided a high level of education for the time.

dignified independence. Remember what happened in the United States when the slaves were suddenly freed by President Lincoln. Many were abruptly reduced to destitution and homelessness by their former owners (who were compensated) who no longer accepted any responsibility for them. They were thrown, without any preparation, into the wider society from which they had been so long excluded by law.

In contrast, observant Muslim masters who embraced their slaves as brothers and sisters encouraged them to work for their freedom, recognized their rights, helped them support a family, and helped them find a place in society before freeing them. The example that comes to mind is that of Zayd ibn Harith, who was brought up in the Prophet's own household and set free. He married a noblewoman and was appointed commander of a Muslim army composed of many noblemen and Companions. There are many similar examples.

There are two important points to emphasize here: the Muslims' attitude toward slavery, and the condition of slaves in non-Muslim countries. Islam considers slavery an accidental and therefore temporary condition, one that is to be reformed step by step until it almost completely disappears. However, it has been observed that some Muslims, especially rulers, continued to hold slaves. Islam cannot be blamed for this, for it is the individual Muslim's own spiritual deficiency that caused him or her to behave in such a manner.

The other point is that personal habits engender a second nature. When Lincoln abolished slavery, most slaves had to return to their former owners because they had never learned how to take the initiative and choose for themselves. As a result, they could not live as free people. Given this psychological reality, prisoners of war were distributed among

Muslims so that one day they could live a true Islamic social life as free people in a Muslim society and enjoy their full legal rights.

Islam sought to abolish slavery gradually. In the first step, it enabled slaves to realize their true human consciousness and identity. After that, it educated them in Islamic and human values, and inculcated in them a love of freedom. Thus, when they were freed, former slaves were equipped to consider all kinds of possibilities related to becoming useful members of the community: farmers, artisans, teachers, scholars, commanders, governors, ministers, or even prime ministers.

Islam attempted to destroy the institution of "individual slavery," and never envisaged or tried "national slavery." So, as a Muslim, I pray to God that enslaved—colonized, oppressed—peoples will enjoy real freedom.

CHAPTER 3

The Qur'an

Did Prophet Muhammad write the Qur'an?

As this question has generated a great deal of literature, I shall confine my answer to the most pertinent points.

This allegation is made by Orientalists,[41] just as it was by their predecessors: Christian and Jewish writers who deeply resented the spread of Islam. The first people to make it were the Prophet's own opponents, as we read in the Qur'an: *Whenever Our signs are recited to them in a clear way, those who deny say concerning the truth, when it (the truth) comes to them: "This is plain magic." Or do they say: "He has forged it."* (46:7-8). They were desperate to protect their interests against the rising tide of Islam and hoped, as do their modern counterparts, to spread doubt about the Qur'an's Divine authorship so that Muslims would start doubting its authority as well.

The Qur'an is unique among Scriptures in two respects, which even its detractors accept. First, the Qur'an exists in Arabic, its original language and one that is still widely spo-

---

[41] Orientalism is an academic discipline that grew out of imperialistic Europe's need to understand and control its Muslim colonies. Its leading figures were usually missionaries or colonial government servants. For more information on the development of Orientalism, see Dr. Edward Said's informative *Orientalism* (Random House: 1979).

ken today. Second, its text is entirely reliable. It has not been altered, edited, or tampered with since it was revealed.

In contrast, Christianity's Gospels have not survived in their original language; the language of the earliest surviving version of these Scriptures is a dead language.[42] In addition, and their texts have been shown to be the work of many people over generations, edited and re-edited, altered and interpolated, to promote sectarian interpretations. They have lost their authority as Scriptures, and serve primarily as a national or cultural mythology for groups whose remote ancestors created their particular versions. This is, more or less, the Western scholarly consensus on the status of these once-Divine Books.

For almost 200 years, Western scholars have subjected the Qur'an to the same rigorous scrutiny. However, they have failed to prove that it was subjected to a similar process. They discovered that Muslims, like Christians, sometimes split into disputing factions. But unlike Christians, all Muslim factions sought to justify their position by referring to the same Qur'an. Other versions of the Gospels might be discovered or uncovered.[43] However, all Muslims know only one Qur'an,

---

[42] According to www.encyclopedia.com, the books dating from the earliest Christian period were transmitted in koiné, a popular form of Greek spoken in the Biblical regions from the 4th century BCE. Modern Greek is quite different. In addition, Christian scholars are not even sure what language Jesus used while teaching (Hebrew, Aramaic, or Greek) or speaking with others.

[43] One wonders why Christian and Jewish scholars have refused, for many years now, to release the text of the Dead Sea scrolls. Might they somehow affect Christian interpretations of certain Biblical passages or ideas?

perfectly preserved in its original words since the Prophet's death, when Revelation ended.[44]

Muslims also have a record of the Prophet's teaching in the Sunna, his implementation of Islam in daily life. Many, but certainly not all, of the Prophet's actions and exact words are preserved in the *hadith* literature.[45] These two sources could not be more dissimilar in quality of expression or content. All Arabs who heard the Prophet speak, regardless of religious

---

[44] In the distant past, some Shi'a groups claimed that Qur'anic verses have been altered or deleted to deprive 'Ali and his descendents of their rightful place in the Islamic world. Tusi, a celebrated Shi'a scholar responsible for two of the Shi'a's *hadith* collections, categorically rejects this assertion, as do the vast majority of Shi'a scholars. Tusi brands all who accept this assertion as unbelievers.

The Qur'an was compiled for the following reason. Shortly after the Prophet died, about 700 Muslims who had memorized the Qur'an were killed while fighting Musaylima the Liar. 'Umar asked Abu Bakr about gathering the various personal records (written on bones, leaves, leather, etc.) to ensure that nothing could be added or deleted. Abu Bakr appointed Zayd ibn Haritha to do this, and the latter compiled the official copy. This copy was checked by those who had memorized the Qur'an. 'Ali did not dispute the official copy's authenticity, nor did he try to change it during his 5-year reign. Recently, several 1,400-year-old Qur'ans were found in Central Asia. When compared with the Qur'an we have today, they were found to be exactly the same.

[45] The study of *hadith* became a very exacting science among Muslim scholars. The *hadith*'s text was checked against the Qur'anic text as well as other *hadith* accepted as authentic. If any inconsistency was found, the *hadith* in question was rejected immediately. Several generations after the Prophet's death, another method of ensuring authenticity was developed: that of studying the lives of those who reported the *hadith*. This science produced a vast amount of biographical literature. If there were any unacceptable breaks in the chain of transmission, or if even one transmitter had one undesirable characteristic, the *hadith* was rejected.

affiliation, found his words to be concise, forceful, and persuasive, but nevertheless like their own normal usage. When they heard the Qur'an, however, they were overwhelmed by feelings of rapture, ecstasy, and awe. One senses in the *hadith* the presence of an individual addressing other people, a man pondering weighty questions who, when he speaks, does so with an appropriate gravity and in profound awe of the Divine Will. The Qur'an, on the other hand, is perceived immediately as imperative and sublime, having a transcendent, all-compelling majesty of style and content. It defies sense and reason to suppose that Qur'an and *hadith* have the same origin.

The Qur'an is absolutely different from any human product in the transcendence of its perspective and viewpoint. Occasionally in a few scattered phrases or passages of other Scriptures, readers or listeners may feel that they are in the presence of the Divine Message addressed to humanity. In the Qur'an, every syllable carries this impression of sublime intensity belonging to a message from One who is All-Knowing and All-Merciful.

Furthermore, the Qur'an cannot be contemplated at a distance, or discussed and debated in the abstract. It requires us to understand, act, and amend our lifestyles. It also enables us to do so, for it can touch us in the very depths of our being. It addresses us in our full reality as spiritually and physically competent beings, as creatures of the All-Merciful. It is not addressed to just one human faculty, such as philosophical reasoning, poetic or artistic sensibility, our ability to alter and manage our environment or political and legal affairs, our need for mutual compassion and forgiveness, or our spiritual craving for knowledge and consolation. The Qur'an also is directed to everyone, regardless of age, gender, race, location, or time.

This transcendence and fullness can be felt in every matter that the Qur'an mentions specifically. For example, caring
for one's elderly parents is placed beside belief in God's
Oneness, and providing decently for a divorced wife with
reminders to be conscious of the All-Knowing and All-
Seeing. While the reasoning behind such placement is God's
alone, His believing servants know and can report its effect:
It enables the inner self-reform that makes the steady, cheer-
ful, and humble performance of virtuous actions possible.
Thus, the one who does the deed does it gracefully, and its
recipient is not oppressed or humiliated by it.

The Qur'an challenges its detractors to compose a chapter that can equal it. No one has successfully met this chal-
lenge. In fact, such an achievement is impossible, for only
God can assume the Qur'an's all-transcendent and all-compassionate perspective. Our thoughts and aspirations are
affected and conditioned by surrounding circumstances. That
is why, sooner or later, all human works fail or fade away into
obsolescence, and why they are too general to have any real
influence or too specific to do much good beyond the specific area they address. Whatever we produce is of limited value
for just these reasons. As stated in the Qur'an: *Say: if all of
humanity and the jinn were to gather together to produce the
like of this Qur'an, they could not produce the like of it, even
if they backed each other with help and support* (17:88).

The Qur'an is the Word of the All-Knowing and All-
Seeing, who knows everything about His creation. It therefore comprehends and tests its audiences as it teaches. For
believers, the consciousness of being before the Divine
Message can make their skins shiver, in the words of the
Qur'an, so suddenly and fully does the atmosphere around
and within them change.

The Qur'an's substance also is a compelling argument for its Divine authorship. Those who allege that someone wrote it provide no proof to support their assertion. Other Scriptures, due to human intervention, make claims that we know to be untrue. For example, they give a particular account of creation or of a natural phenomenon (e.g., the Flood), which we know from modern scientific facts, such as fossils or astronomic discoveries, to be false. People altered those Scriptures to suit their own understanding, with the result that the progress of science has rendered their understanding and their now-corrupted Scriptures largely irrelevant and obsolete. However, the Qur'an has not been subject to such mistreatment.

If someone wrote the Qur'an, how could it be literally true on matters that were completely unknown at the time of its revelation? *Do not the unbelievers realize that the Heavens and the Earth were one unit of creation before we split them asunder?* (21:30). Only in the last few years have we been able to contemplate this verse about the first moment of the universe in its literal meaning.

Similarly, when we now read: *God raised the Heavens without any pillars that you can see. Then He established Himself on the throne [of authority]. He has subjected the sun and moon [to a law]; each runs its course for a term appointed. He regulate all affairs, explaining the signs in detail, that you may believe certainly in the meeting with your Lord* (13:2), now we can understand the invisible pillars as the vast centrifugal and centripetal forces maintaining the balance amid the heavenly bodies. We also understand from this and related verses (e.g., 55:5; 21:33, 38, 39; and 36:40) that the sun and moon are stars with a fixed life-span, that their force of light has or will fade away, and that they follow an orbit that has been determined with the most minute exactness.

A literal understanding of these verses does not diminish the responsibility that comes with understanding—*that you may believe certainly in the meeting with your Lord.* The purpose of the verses has not changed; only our knowledge of the phenomenal world has changed. In the case of former Scriptures, scientific progress has made their inaccuracies ever more visible and their associated beliefs ever more irrelevant. Just the opposite is true with the Qur'an—scientific progress has not made even a single verse harder to believe or to understand. On the contrary, such progress had made many verses more understandable.

Yet some people still allege that the Prophet wrote the Qur'an. While asserting that they are on the side of sense and reason, they allege what is humanly impossible. How could a seventh-century man know things that only recently have been accepted as scientifically established truths? How is that humanly possible? How is it on the side of reason and sense to claim such a thing? How did the Prophet discover, with an anatomical and biological accuracy only recently confirmed, that milk is produced in mammal tissues? How did he discover how rain clouds and hailstones form, or determine a wind's fertilizing quality, or explain how landmasses shift and continents form and reform? With what giant telescope did he learn of the universe's ongoing physical expansion? By what equivalent of X-ray vision was he able to describe in such great detail the different stages of an embryo's evolution within the uterus?

Another proof of the Qur'an's Divine origin is that what it predicts eventually comes true. For example, the Companions considered the Treaty of Hudaibiyya a defeat; the Revelation stated that they would enter the Sacred Mosque in full security and that Islam would prevail over all other religions (48:27-28). It also promised that the Romans

[Byzantines] would vanquish the Persians several years after their utter defeat in 615, and that the Muslims would destroy both of these current superpowers (30:2-5), at a time when there were scarcely 40 believers, all of whom were being persecuted by the Makkan chiefs.

Although the Prophet was the ideal man, he could make mistakes on matters not related to Islam or Revelation. For example:

- When he exempted certain hypocrites from jihad, he was criticized: *God forgive you! Why did you let them stay behind before it became clear which of them were truthful and which were liars?* (9:43).

- After the Battle of Badr, he was rebuked: *You (the believers) merely seek the gains of the world whereas God desires [for you the good] of the Hereafter. God is All-Mighty, All-Wise. Had there not been a previous decree from God, a stern punishment would have afflicted you for what you have taken...*(8:67-68).

- Once he said he would do something the next day and did not say "if God wills." He was warned: *Nor say of anything, I shall be sure to do so-and-so tomorrow, without adding "if God wills." Call your Lord to mind when you forget, and say: "I hope that my Lord will guide me ever closer than this to the right way"* (18:23-24), and *You feared the people, but God has a better right that you should fear Him* (33:37).

- When he swore that he would never again use honey or drink a honey-based sherbet, he was admonished: *O Prophet. Why do you hold to be forbidden what God has made lawful to you? You seek to please your wives. But God is Oft-Forgiving, Most Merciful* (66:1).

In other verses, when the Prophet's higher duties and responsibilities are brought into clear focus, the limits to his authority are made known. There is a clear space between the Messenger and the Message revealed to him, as clear as between a person and his or her Creator.

Orientalists deny the Divine authorship out of fear of Islam. Many miracles are associated with the Qur'an. One of the clearest is how quickly it established a distinctive and enduring civilization by serving as its constitution and framework. It mandated the administrative, legal, and fiscal reforms necessary to sustain a vast state of different cultural communities and religions. The Qur'an inspired a genuinely scientific curiosity to study nature and travel in order to study different peoples and cultures. By urging people to lend money for commercial ventures and to abandon interest, it made sure that the community's growing wealth would circulate. It inspired the first-ever public literacy and public hygiene programs, as both were necessary for worship. The Qur'an also commanded the organized redistribution of surplus wealth to the poor and needy, to widows and orphans, for the relief of captives and debtors, the freeing of slaves, and for the support of new Muslims.

One could expand this list considerably, for only the Qur'an has ever achieved what many people have desired. Do we not know of at least one human idea of how to establish or run an ideal society, at least one system or formula for solving equitably social, cultural, or political problems? Have any of them ever worked or lasted?

Those who deny the Qur'an's Divine authorship also fear its power and authority, and that some day Muslims might obey its commands and restore their civilization. They would prefer that the Muslim elite, as well as other Muslims, believe that the Qur'an is a human work belonging to a certain time and place, and therefore no longer relevant. Such a belief would relegate Islam to Christianity's current status: a tender memory of something long gone.

Such people want Muslims to believe that the Qur'an belongs to the seventh century. They admit, in order to beguile Muslims, that the Qur'an was very advanced for its time. However, now they are the ones who are advanced, who offer a lifestyle of intellectual and cultural freedom, and who are civilized, whereas the Qur'an and Islam are backward. But, scientific progress proves the Qur'an's accuracy on questions related to the phenomenal world and helps us to better understand the Qur'an, just as improvements in our understanding of human relationships and human psychology will establish its truth in these areas.

Claiming that a person wrote the Qur'an only reflects the failure to understand that all individuals are indebted to God, Who has given us everything. We do not create ourselves, for our lives are given to us, as are our abilities to contemplate, comprehend, and feel compassion. We are given this extraordinarily subtle, varied, and renewable world to exercise these abilities. In addition, the Qur'an is a gift of mercy, for there is no way it could have had a human author.

Why was the Qur'an revealed over a period of 23 years?

Before I answer this question, let's note that if the Qur'an had been revealed all at once, people would ask: "Why was it sent down all at once and not in stages?" The ultimate answer to such questions lies with God, the All-Wise and All-Knowing. Our decisions are based on a very limited viewpoint, as we are limited creatures. The Divine Decree, on the other hand, considers everything—our moral and spiritual well-being, worldly happiness, future and present—and weaves the whole into a single pattern that is coherent with Grace and Wisdom. Thus, the benefit we derive from the Divine commandments is immeasurable, and the blessing that flows from obeying them is beyond our imagination. And so it is with the method that God chose to reveal the Qur'an.

The Revelation began when it was time for humanity to reach maturity. The Prophet's mission and that of his community was to become the most complete, progressive, and dynamic exemplars for humanity, and to achieve such a level of advancement that they would be the masters and guides for all subsequent people. But these reformers first had to be reformed. Their qualities and characters had been conditioned by the surrounding non-Islamic environment in which their people had been living for centuries. Islam was to turn their good qualities into qualities of unsurpassed excellence, and to purge their bad qualities and habits in such a way that they would never reappear.

If the Qur'an had been revealed all at once, how would they have reacted to its prohibitions and commandments? Certainly, they would have been unable to understand, let alone accept and apply, them in the ideal manner. This lack of gradualism would have been self-defeating, as proven by history: Wherever Islam was taken, it spread gradually but steadily, and so became firmly established.

We see people all around us who cannot free themselves from their bad habits and addictions. If you confined such people, even if you convinced them to abandon their habits for their own benefit, they would not be happy with you. On the contrary, they would feel angry, bored, and irritated. They would complain and try to escape from your program of reform, so that they could revert to their habits as soon as possible. All the arguments and documented evidence of specialists and experts would not persuade them to change. Even those who were cured occasionally suffer a relapse. Indeed, some of those who campaign against such harmful habits as smoking and consuming alcohol still indulge in them!

Remember that the Qur'an came to change not one or two habits; it came to change everything: ways of living and dying, marrying, buying and selling, settling disputes, and how to perceive one's relation with the Creator, among others. Given the scope of the change envisioned, we can begin to grasp why it was revealed in stages.

The gradual revelation of the Qur'an prepared the people to accept and then live the virtues, excellent manners, and lofty aspirations it demanded. That so much was achieved in only 23 years is a miracle. As Said Nursi said: "I wonder if the scholars of today went to the Arabian peninsula, could they accomplish in 100 years even 1 percent of what the Prophet accomplished in 1 year?" Current campaigns to eradicate such a peripheral vice as smoking employ famous scholars, individuals, institutions, and the whole network of mass media—yet they still result in overall failure. If 20 fewer people die on the road per year after a campaign against alcohol, it is considered a great success. What the Prophet accomplished, at God's bidding, over 23 years far surpasses what all of humanity has managed to achieve since that time.

The Qur'an was revealed in stages so that its audience could understand, internalize, and apply its prohibitions, commands, and reforms. Revelation came when the need for guidance arose, without discouraging or grinding down morale: warning and condemnation preceded prohibition, appeal and exhortation preceded command. For instance, alcohol and other intoxicating drinks were prohibited in three or four stages; female infanticide in two stages; uniting warring tribes and building up a close-knit society based on brotherhood, thus raising the collective consciousness, in several stages. These difficult reforms were not gestured at or expressed in slogans—they were achieved.

Today, we design our projects according to past experience and future possibilities. Taking possible social and economic fluctuations into account, we make our plans flexible in order to leave room for any necessary modifications. Just like a young tree, the early Muslims grew slowly, adapting gradually to new conditions and thus developing naturally. Every day new people were coming into Islam. New Muslims were learning many things, gaining in Islamic consciousness, training themselves to act upon Islam, and thus becoming members of a society rather than separate individuals or mutually hostile clans. Their characters and personalities, their whole lives, were reshaped and reordered in accordance with Islamic precepts and the Qur'anic guidance.

Such was the magnitude of their spiritual, moral, intellectual, and even physical regeneration. This transformation was achieved through a balanced synthesis of worldly life and spiritual advancement, and it happened gradually, slowly yet continuously, and harmoniously.

Why does the Qur'an open with *iqra'* (recite, read)?

The Divine command to proclaim Islam opens with the sublime imperative: *iqra'*. Usually translated as "recite," it also means to "rehearse aloud" or to "read." It is addressed to humanity, as the Prophet represents humanity in its relationship to God. *Iqra'* is thus a universal injunction, an opening for each individual to move away from imperfection and toward virtue and happiness both in this world and the next.

Iqra' is a command to *read* the signs the Creator placed in creation so that we can understand something of His Mercy, Wisdom, and Power. It is a command to learn, through experience and understanding, the meaning of His creation. Moreover, it is an infallible assurance that the creation can be read, that it is *intelligible.* The better we learn to read it, the better we grasp that the created world is a single universe whose beauty and harmony reflect the Guarded Tablet (85:21) upon which, by the Divine decree, all things are inscribed.

Every created thing resembles a pen that records its actions. But only humanity can read what is written. That is why the Qur'an tells us to "read" instead of to "behold." We are to know the creation, not just to experience it, as is the case with all other creations.

Science is the study of nature, of how the universe functions, and of the harmony and principles governing all interactions. It accumulates knowledge via observation and classification, explanation and experiment. The balanced order, delicate interrelatedness, and prolific dynamism thereof cannot be attributed to chance. Logic dictates that a Single, Supreme Being created and sustains all of this.

Every order or system is conceived and designed before it is established. Think of the Guarded Tablet as a detailed design, and the Qur'an as its verbal exposition. Given this, the universe may be considered a reflection in our world of that final design. We hardly can think of creation as a single universe, let alone conceive of a design and then produce one. Our duty is to read it and seek the full meaning of everything. We do this through trial and error, for that is the only way we can learn.

What sort of knowledge are we trying to acquire? There are many types of knowledge and understanding: that based on beholding or actively seeing something, inner (comprehensive knowledge) or outer (description and measurement), implementation of the lesser understanding (technology) or of the spiritual understanding (contemplation and worship, which yield wisdom), learning and teaching, self-based or other-based, the learner's or teacher's belief in independence of action or being, and of the believer's surrender and trust to the Creator.

Such diversity happens side by side and continually, for the universe contains certain laws and categories that condition all being and action within it. These laws and categories are placed therein by the Creator, Who administers and sustains their harmonious operation. Among them are the following:

- A movement from one to many, from simplicity to complexity

- A process of becoming, the coming into existence (within the many) of similar, diverse, or opposed elements

- A dynamic, enduring balance among the many

- Succession or alternation, the transfer of property, vigor, power, or knowledge from one to another

- Acquisition, loss, and reacquisition, or learning, forgetting, and relearning

- Striving and persevering, or energy and commitment

- Breaking down and recomposition, or analysis and synthesis

- Inspiration that uncovers and reveals, or intuition that pierces and makes clear.

Since humanity is subject to these and other conditions, people are very diverse in all aspects. However, as these natural differences and contrasts are in a dynamic, prolific balance, people have different (and changing) conceptions of and approaches to such matters as science and faith.

As a result of such diversity, some teachings—even those of the Prophet—may be lost sight of for a time. But one day they will be recollected and taught again. After such a large increase in the number and variety of people, the loss of traditions and histories, as well as fragmentation, is natural. All of these will be repaired, though, for this process has happened many times in the past and will happen again in the future.

Divinely inspired Scriptures, Prophets, and laws were sent successively, in part as an assurance of this process. The Prophet was blessed with a character that harmonized something of the distinguishing excellence of all previous Prophets. In him were blended the most profound spiritual knowledge and wisdom, the will to move and decisively order collective affairs, to inspire human hearts and direct their spiritual craving, to heal differences between people, and to achieve lasting reconciliation. He demonstrated the ideal balance, in individual as well as in collective affairs, between the claims of justice and compassion. His life is full of suffering, forbearance, steadfastness in defeat, and of relief, success, and victory. His style of expression was always brief, to the point, memorable, and perfect. Alongside the Qur'an, he was the fountainhead of a spiritual awakening and of a great and enduring civilization.

That is why responding to *iqra'* means wider responsibilities and a greater degree of inner and outer trial and striving for Muslims than for members of other religions. This greater trial is a means of grace and honor, for it enables a richer harmony of more diverse virtues in each Muslim and in the community.

Recent scientific discoveries have clarified certain Qur'anic verses. Such advances in knowledge occur successively, as the universe proceeds upon its decreed course and in the measure of understanding appointed for us. We must acknowledge and praise the efforts and achievements of researchers and scientists, but they should not lead us to ingratitude and insolence (the roots of unbelief). Rather, we should reaffirm our dependence upon the Creator for guidance both in our quest for and application of knowledge. We must not idolize ourselves, lest we be forsaken and left with the human will to power as the only judge in our affairs.

Should that happen, scientific research and achievement will remain with those who seek to use them for their own temporary advantage. Science will become a weapon against religion, a helpless servant of selfish and generally atheistic and materialistic ideologies. The end result might be an irretrievable degradation in the quality of individual and community life. We can see all around us that applying new technologies is making more and more people increasingly impatient, arrogant, irresponsible, and hard-hearted. Some even claim that they are answerable only to themselves, as if they were self-created! And yet their lives remain full of unhappiness, stress, anxiety, unsatisfied needs, and the delusion that they are free.

The sheer pace of the current scientific advance has turned human societies and individuals into laboratory experiments with no sure knowledge of the consequences or final outcome. To counteract this, we must see that the Divine command of *iqra'* is reunited with contemplation, that we relearn how to "read" consciously so that we can acquire true understanding and wisdom.

If we can do this, we will begin to deliver science from the futility and dry formalism in which it is bound, and help to clarify its philosophical foundations and social and moral relevance. We also will be able to indicate the true range of human perception, intellect, and intuition, and make people aware of their proper balance and use. Then, those who consciously study creation will read its signs with a religious seriousness and humility, and will acquire knowledge that is civilizing and beneficial for humanity.

That we are meant to read in this way and for this purpose is beyond doubt. The first thing created was the Pen, and the first word of the Revelation was *iqra'*.[46] But to read in such a way requires that our inner and outer faculties be alert and harmoniously directed to the phenomena. Any defect in our inner faculties impacts the proper functioning of the others.

When referring to a malaise of the spirit, the Qur'an speaks of blindness, deafness, and dumbness. The Creator's signs are first "read" with the eyes. The first sounds of Revelation are "heard" with the ears, which then channels them to the understanding. All that is seen and heard is expounded, interpreted, and communicated by the tongue, so that understanding can be deepened.

If people have a poor inner life, they will be able to see, hear, or give voice to only that which affects their immediate survival or pleasure. Reading the signs will be impossible, for they will see only mechanically related bodies and surfaces, and their minds will focus on the rules and laws that will

---

[46] Ibn Hanbal, *Musnad,* 5:317; Abu Dawud, *Sunan,* 16; Tirmidhi, *Qadar,* 17.

place them under control. As their inner life atrophies, contemplation and compassion will be replaced by ugliness, triviality, and barbarism. Left to themselves, such people will master neither their immediate needs and pleasures, nor their constant insecurity, anxiety, and dissatisfaction. In truth, they are blind, deaf, and dumb, and the universe is no more than a narrow prison for them.

Why does the Qur'an not discuss scientific issues that concern us today?

The Qur'an was revealed for specific purposes: to make us aware of the Creator, to affirm that He is known through His creation, to direct us to belief and worship, and to order individual and collective life so that we attain real happiness here and in the Hereafter. The Qur'an deals with each subject according to the importance attached to it by God.

Given the above reasons, the Qur'an is comprehensive. This can be seen by the countless books and commentaries written about its various aspects. The perfection of its style and eloquence has been attested to by the greatest Muslim literary masters of every century, and has inspired them to excellence not only in Arabic but also in other Islamic languages. By basing themselves on Islam, Muslim scholars of humanity or the physical world have been able to comprehend the real nature of things and events. Through the Qur'an's wisdom, psychologists and sociologists have resolved the thorniest problems related to individual or collective affairs. Moralists and pedagogues have turned to the Qur'an as an infinite, inexhaustible resource for educating future generations.

Today, many people want to know what the Qur'an says about scientific and technological matters, and how it relates to modern positive sciences. Many books have been written on this subject. They have tried to relate Qur'anic truths to advances in scientific knowledge. Many of these books were influenced by the culture and science of their time. But despite the care and pains expended on these commentaries, people doubt their accuracy and find them overelaborate and far-fetched. In particular, efforts to make Qur'anic truths correspond to particular scientific hypotheses appear to distort, misrepresent, and even slight the Qur'an.

When explaining the Qur'an, we must be objective and remain faithful to its precision, soundness, and clarity. Instead of interpreting it in the light of certain phenomena and a non-Qur'anic specialist language, everything should be interpreted and evaluated in the Qur'anic context. Of course, the Qur'an is best understood by a nuanced knowledge of Arabic's vocabulary and grammatical rules, and the occasions of the verse's revelation. Thus the best understanding and interpretation is that of the Companions, then of the Successors (the following generation), and then of the first commentators, such as Ibn Jarir. These, and not the later ones, are the most in accord with scientific truths established later on.

We offer several examples from the Qur'an to illustrate the argument.

- The Omnipotent Creator says that the future will be the age of knowledge and information, and thus, as a natural consequence, of faith and belief: *Soon We shall show them Our signs on the furthest horizons, and in their own souls, until it becomes manifest to them that this is truth. Is it not enough that your Lord witnesses all things?* (41:53).

From the earliest days of Islam, Sufis accepted and referred to this verse as a sign and assurance of the spiritual wisdom they sought.[47] However, reading this verse from the viewpoint of scientific progress, its mere existence will be seen to be a miracle.

Everything within the compass of our thinking and research affirms the Creator's Oneness, as the true nature and interrelationship of microcosm and macrocosm are further disclosed and better understood. When we see hundreds of books on this subject, we understand that what was Divinely revealed is near to being proved. Even now we feel that soon we shall hear and be able to understand the testimonies and praises to God through thousands of tongues belonging to nature: *The seven Heavens and the Earth, and all things therein, declare His Glory. There is not a thing but celebrates His praise. And yet you do not understand how they declare His Glory. Truly He is Oft-Forbearing, Most Forgiving* (17:44).

This verse tells us that all parts of creation speak to us, in the language of their being, of their submission to and glorification of the One God. However, very few people can hear and understand this universal praise. The sincere Muslims who will bring all people to hear this praise are also few, dispersed, and feeble.

- What the Qur'an reveals about an embryo's formation and developmental phases in the uterus is striking: *O mankind! If you have a doubt about the Resurrection, (consider) that We created you out of dust, then out of*

---

[47] Sufis represent the mystical and inner spiritual dimension of Islam. For more information on this fascinating field, please consult the works of Annemarie Schimmel, Martin Lings, Idries Shah, Henry Corbin, Sheikh Nazim al-Haqqani an-Naqshbandiyya, Louis Massignon, Jalal Al-Din Rumi, William C. Chittick, Seyyed Hossein Nasr, Fethullah Gülen, and many others.

sperm, then out of a leech-like cloth, then out of a lump of flesh, partly formed and partly unformed, in order that We may manifest (what We will) to you... (22:5)

In another verse, the development is explained in greater detail, and the distinct phases are emphasized more clearly:

> We created man from a quintessence (of clay). Then We placed him as (a drop of) sperm in a place of rest, firmly fixed. Then we made the sperm into a clot of congealed blood. Then of that clot We made a lump (embryo); then we made out of that lump bones and clothed the bones with flesh. Then We developed out of it a new (distinct, individual) creature (23:12-14)

And

> He makes you in the wombs of your mothers in stages, one after another, in three veils of darkness ... (39:6)

These three veils of darkness can now be glossed in detail: the parametrium, miometrium, and the endometrium are three tissues enveloping three water-, heat-, and light-proof membranes (the amnion, corion and the wall of the womb).

• What the Qur'an says about milk and its production: *And verily in cattle (too) will you find an instructive sign. From what is from their bodies, between excretions and blood, We produce, for your drink, milk, pure and agreeable to those who drink it* (16:66).

The Qur'an narrates the process in remarkable detail: the partial digestion of food and its absorption, followed by a second process and refinement in the glands. Milk is wholesome and agreeable for people, yet it is a secretion rejected by the cow's body and bloodstream as useless.

• The Qur'an reveals that all things in nature are created in pairs: *Glory be to God, who created in pairs all things, of what the soil produces, and of themselves, and of what they know not* (36:36).

Thus everything has a counterpart, whether opposite to it or complementary. This is obvious in the case of people, animals, and certain plants. But, what about the pairs in *all things ... and of what they know not?* This may refer to a whole range of inanimate as well as animate entities, subtle forces and principles of nature. Modern scientific instruments confirm that everything does occur in pairs.

• The Qur'an recounts, in its own unique idiom, the first creation of the world and its inhabitants: *Do not the unbelievers see that the Heavens and the Earth were joined together (as a single mass), before We clove them asunder? We made from water every living thing. Will they not then believe?* (21:30).

The Qur'anic account is clear and should not be mixed with the different creation hypotheses put forward by others. It states that every living thing was created of water. The Qur'an does not concern itself with how this unique source of life came into being, but with the fact that the universe is a single miracle of creation. Everything in it is an integral part of that miracle, bears signs that prove it, and is interconnected. The verse emphasizes the vitality and significance of water, which constitutes three-quarters of the mass of most living bodies.

• The sun has a special and significant place in creation. The Qur'an reveals its most important aspects in just four words: *And the sun runs its course* (mustaqarr) *determined for it. That is His decree, the Exalted in Might, the All-Knowing* (36:38).

In fact, *mustaqarr* here may mean a determined route in space, a fixed place of rest or dwelling, or a determined route in time. We are told that the sun has a specific orbit and that it moves toward a particular point in the universe. Our solar system, as we now know, is moving toward the constellation Lyra at an almost inconceivable speed (every second we come ten miles closer to that constellation, almost a million miles a day). We also are told that when the sun has finished its appointed task, it will abide by a command and come to rest.

Such words were spoken at a time when people generally believed that the sun made a daily circuit around the Earth.

• Another four-word inspiring and eloquent Qur'anic verse says that the universe is expanding: *And the firmament: We constructed it with power and skill, and We are expanding it* (51:47-48).

This verse reveals that the distance between celestial bodies is increasing, for the universe is expanding. In 1922, the astronomer Hubble claimed that all galaxies, except the five closest to Earth, are moving further into space at a speed directly proportional to their distance from Earth. Thus, a galaxy one million light years away is moving away at a speed of 168 km/year, one two million light years away at twice that speed, and so on. Le Maître, a Belgian mathematician and priest, later proposed and developed the theory that the universe is expanding. No matter how we express this reality, the Qur'an clearly presents the reality of this expansion.

• The Qur'an indicates various laws of physics, such as attraction and repulsion, rotation and revolution in the universe: *God raised the heavens without any pillars that you can see...* (13:2)

All celestial bodies move in order, balance, and harmony. They are held and supported in this order by pillars invisible to our eyes. Some of these "pillars" are repulsion or centrifugal force: ... *He holds back the sky from falling on earth except by His leave...* (22:65).

From this verse, we understand that the heavenly bodies may at any moment collapse on the Earth, but that the All-Mighty does not allow it. This is an instance of the universal obedience to His Word, which in the language of contemporary science is explained as a balance of centripetal and centrifugal forces.

• Qur'anic commentators have considered one verse as a reference to travelling to the moon, which is now a reality: *By the moon's fullness! You shall surely travel from stage to stage* (84:18-19).

Some earlier commentators understood this verse figuratively, as a reference to one's spiritual life considered as an ascent from one stage to the next, or as a general process of change from one state to another. Later on, Qur'anic interpreters tried to explain it in non-literal terms, for the literal meaning did not agree with what they "knew" about actually travelling such a distance. But in fact, the more appropriate sense of the words following the oath (*By the moon!*), given the verse's immediate context, is that of really travelling to the moon, whether literally or figuratively.

• The Qur'anic account of the Earth's geographical shape and change in that shape are particularly interesting: *Do they not see how We gradually shrink the land from its outlying borders? Is it then they who will be victors?* (21:44).

The reference to shrinking from its borders could relate to the now-known fact that the Earth is compressed at the poles, rather than to such earlier believed ideas as the erosion of mountains by wind and rain, of the sea-shores by the sea, or of the desert's encroachment of cultivated lands.

At a time when people generally believed that the Earth was flat and stationary, the Qur'an explicitly and implicitly revealed in several verses that it is round. More unexpectedly still, it tells us that its precise shape is more like an ostrich egg than a sphere: *After that He shaped the earth like an egg, whence He caused to spring forth the water thereof, and the pasture thereof* (79:30-32).

The Arabic verb *daha* means "to shape like an egg." The derived noun *dahia* is still used to mean "an egg." Some interpreters, who might have viewed it as contrary to what they "knew," misunderstood the meaning as "stretched out," perhaps fearing that the literal meaning might be difficult to understand and so mislead. Modern scientists have established that the Earth is shaped more like an egg than a perfect sphere, that there is a slight flattening around the poles, and a slight curving around the equator.

• As a final example, consider what the Qur'an says about the sun and the moon: *We have made the night and the day as two signs; the sign of the night We have obscured, while the sign of the day We have made to enlighten you...* (17:12).

According to Ibn 'Abbas, *the sign of the night* refers to the moon, and *the sign of the day* to the sun. Therefore, from the words *the sign of the night We have obscured*, we understand that the moon once emitted light and that God took its light from it, thereby causing it to darken or become obscured. While the verse thus accurately recounts the moon's past, it points to the future destiny of other heavenly bodies.

Many other Qur'anic verses are related to scientific facts. Their existence indicates that our quest for knowledge is a portion of Divine Mercy graciously bestowed upon us by our Creator. Indeed, Divine Mercy is one of the Qur'an's names for itself, and all that it contains of truth and knowledge is beyond our ability to relate or to hold in our minds.

We must remember, however, that while the Qur'an contains allusions to many scientific truths, it is not a science textbook. It is a book of guidance leading humanity to right belief and right action so that we may be worthy of Divine Mercy and Forgiveness. Muslims must ensure that the pursuit of scientific and other types of knowledge is guided by the light of the Qur'an, which so encourages and supports it, and not by the spirit of arrogance, insolence, and vainglory. The latter path, that of unbelievers, leads only to the mind's desolation, our own degradation and that of the Earth, our temporary home entrusted to us by God.

When modern science agrees with the Qur'an

We refer to many branches of science and scientific facts today and use them to analyze various things and events— even religious matters. We refer to them, either one at a time or in groups, to provide evidence of God's Existence and Oneness to those who need such evidence.

Similarly, when looking at science in the light of the Qur'an, we point out that it contains information about the nature of things that agrees with modern scientific findings. Consider medicine. I once read a book called *Medicine is the Niche of the Faith*. It really is so, and we must acknowledge

God when studying our bodily existence and development. For instance, the Qur'anic description of the embryo corresponds exactly to what we know today. Furthermore, the Qur'an does not contain a single statement on this matter that modern science can criticize. How could an unlettered desert Arab living more than 1,400 years ago know such facts, which were discovered recently by X-rays and other sophisticated equipment only after many centuries of intensive scientific research? We use such Qur'anic statements to argue for the Qur'an's Divine origin. This, in turn, corroborates the truth of Muhammad's Prophethood.

We refer to science and scientific facts when explaining Islam because some people are determined to reject anything that is not "scientific." Materialists and those opposed (or indifferent) to religion have sought to exploit science to defy religion and use its prestige to spread their thinking. Many people have followed their lead, which means that we have to use the same tools of science and technology to show that they do not contradict Islam and to lead people to the right path.

I agree with such an argument. Muslims should be well-versed in scientific facts to refute the claims of materialists and atheists. Many Qur'anic verses urge us to reflect and study, to observe the stars and galaxies. They impress upon us the Creator's magnificence, and exhort us to travel and observe the miraculousness of our organs and creation. The Qur'an's verses place all of creation before our eyes. Touching upon a multitude of facts, it tells us that *those who truly fear God, among His servants, are those who have knowledge* (35:28), and so encourages us to seek knowledge,[48]

---

[48] In Islamic terms, knowledge is not restricted to religious knowledge, but includes all types of knowledge beneficial to humanity. For us, this certainly includes scientific knowledge.

to reflect and research. However, remember that the first condition for all such activities is that they comply with the spirit of the Qur'an, lest we begin departing from it.

Our knowledge of science and its facts can and should be used to expound Islamic facts, not to impress others or silence their arguments. Our primary aim must be to win the pleasure of God and make sure that our audience understands the points we are making.

It is wrong to regard science as superior to religion and to seek to justify substantial Islamic issues and Islam as a whole through modern scientific facts. Such attempts show that we have doubts about Islam and thus need science to reinforce our own belief. It is also wrong to accept science or scientific facts as absolute, for such things are subject to change. At best, they only support what the Qur'an says. In no way can the unchangeable and eternal Qur'an be confirmed by that which is changeable and temporary. Given this, Muslims should use science only as a tool to awaken sleeping or confused minds.

Science and scientific facts are true only as long as they agree with the Qur'an and *hadith*. Even definitely established scientific facts cannot uphold the truths of faith; they can be only instruments to give us ideas or to trigger us to reflect. God, not science, establishes the truths of faith in our conscience, for faith comes only by Divine guidance. Those who seek to acquire faith from science may never feel the existence of God within their own consciousness. In reality, they will be nature worshippers, not worshippers of God.

We are believers because of the faith in our hearts, not the knowledge in our heads. Objective and subjective evidence can take us only so far. After that, we must drop all such things in order to make any spiritual progress at all. When we follow our heart and conscience within the Qur'an's light and guidance, God may guide us to the enlightenment for which we are looking. As the German philosopher Kant said: "I felt the need to leave behind all the books I read in order to believe in God."

CHAPTER 4

Prophethood and Prophets

What is the role of Prophethood and of Prophets?

Prophethood is the highest rank and honor that a man can receive from God. It proves the superiority of that man's inner being over all others. A Prophet is like a branch arching out from the Divine to the human realm. He is the very heart and tongue of creation. He possesses a supreme intellect that penetrates into the reality of things and events.

Moreover, he is the ideal being, for *all* of his faculties are harmoniously excellent and active. He strives and progresses steadily toward Heaven, waits upon Divine inspiration for the solutions to the problems he faces, and is the connecting point between this world and the Beyond. His body is subject to and follows his heart, figuratively the seat of spiritual intellect, as does his heart. His perceptions and reflections are always directed to the Names and Attributes of God. He goes to what he perceives, and arrives at the desired destination.

A Prophet's perception, developed to the full—seeing, hearing, and thus knowing—surpasses that of all other people. His perception cannot be explained in terms of different light, sound, or some other wavelengths. Ordinary people cannot acquire a Prophet's knowledge.

By conveying the Divine message and guidance, the Prophets give us a limited insight into creation so that we can know some of its meaning. Without them, we would be unable to see or understand the true nature and meaning of things and events, or to deal with our surrounding environment. They also teach us something of God and His Names and Attributes.

Their first mission is to teach the reality, the true purpose and meaning, of this life. Since God is beyond our perception and comprehension, the Prophets have to be the most obedient, careful, conscious, and self-disciplined of people while performing their tasks. If they had not spoken in clear terms about the Creator, we could not think, know, or say anything correct about God.

Everything in the universe tries to exhibit the Names and Attributes of the All-Mighty, All-Encompassing Creator. In the same way, the Prophets note, affirm, and are faithful to the subtle, mysterious relation between God and His Names and Attributes. As their duty is to know and speak about God, they enter into the true meaning of things and events and then convey it directly and sincerely to humanity.

When we are in a new or unfamiliar place, we need a guide. This analogy applies to the role of Prophets. Would the One who created everything so that we might know Him not provide guides, in the form of Prophets, to inform us of His Names and Attributes and guide us along the right path? To overlook such a need would render the creation useless and futile, yet we know that God does not engage in such activities. Thus, it seems most likely that all people would be informed of such things by a Prophet sent to them by God.

The Qur'an is explicit on this point: *For We sent among every people a Messenger (with the command): "Serve God and avoid evil"* (16:36). But many people gradually forgot these Divine teachings and fell into such errors as deifying the Prophets and others or engaging in idolatry. We can see this in the deities of Mt. Olympus in ancient Greece, the sanctification of the Ganges river in India, and in many other places. Even accepting that there must be a tremendous difference between the original and the current form of many religions, it is quite impossible to understand the conditions that caused Confucius to appear in China and Brahma and Buddha in India. It is equally difficult to guess what their original messages were and to what degree they have been corrupted.

If the Qur'an had not introduced Jesus to us, we would not have an accurate idea of his life and teachings. Over time, priests (and others) mixed the truth of Jesus with ancient Greek and Roman philosophies and idolatry, attributed divinity to human beings, and anthropomorphized God. The Trinity is an obvious example. Perhaps Rome would accept Christianity as its official state religion only if the various pagan festivals, holy days, rites, and rituals were incorporated. Without the Qur'an's enlightening revelation, it would be very difficult to tell Jesus Christ from Adonis or Dionysus.[49]

Considering that Christianity is relatively recent, and what the Christians did to their Prophet and their Book, we wonder how many other people fell into the same error. One reliable hadith says: "A Prophet's disciples will carry out his mission after his death, but some of his followers will later upset everything he established."[50] This is a very important

---

[49] Two originally ancient Greek "gods" that were widely worshipped in Greece and those lands under its cultural sway, as well as in the Roman Empire.

[50] Muslim, *Fada'il al-Sahaba*, 210-12; Ibn Hanbal, *Musnad*, 417.

point. Many of the religions we now consider false turned to falsehood, superstition, and legend over time through the deliberate malice of their enemies (or the mistakes of their followers), despite their possible origin in the purest, Divine source.

To say that someone is a Prophet when he is not is unbelief, as is the case with refusing to believe in a true Prophet. On the other hand, if the case of false religions is similar to that of Christianity, we should look at them with some caution and reserve judgment. We should consider what Buddhism or Brahmanism may have been in their true, original forms, as well as the doctrines attributed to Confucius or the practices and beliefs of shamanism. Maybe they still have some remnants of what they originally were.

Many once-pure religions have been distorted and altered. Therefore, it is essential to accept the purity of their original foundation. The Qur'an says: *There never was a people without a warner having lived among them* (35:24), and *We sent among every people a Messenger* (16:36).

These revelations declare that God sent Messengers to each group of people. The Qur'an mentions the names of 28 Prophets, out of a total of 124,000 (or perhaps 224,000). We do not know exactly when and where many of them lived. But we do not have to know such information, for: *We did in times past send Messengers before you; of them there are some whose stories We have related to you, and some whose stories We have not related to you* (40:78).

Recent studies in comparative religion, philosophy, and anthropology reveal that many widely separated communities share certain concepts and practices. Among these are moving from polytheism to monotheism, and praying to the One God in times of hardship by raising their hands and asking something from Him. Many such phenomena indicate a singular source and a single teaching. If primitive tribes cut off from civilization and the influence of known Prophets have a sure understanding of His Oneness, though they may have little understanding of how to live according to that belief, a Messenger must have been sent to them at some time in the past: *For every people there is a Messenger. When their Messenger comes, the matter is judged between them with justice, and they are not wronged* (10:47).

What about those who claim to have been sent no Prophet? Are they held accountable for their beliefs and actions? According to the verse quoted above, a Prophet has been sent to every people. There may be periods when darkness seemed to prevail, but such periods are only temporary. Nevertheless, there is the possibility that the Prophet's work was destroyed so completely by erroneous ideas and rites that the true teachings were lost. In such cases, people may have remained in darkness unknowingly or against their own will. Such people will not be punished or blamed for the wrong they may do, until and unless they have been warned: *We never punish until We have sent a Messenger* (17:15), for warning precedes responsibility and reward or punishment.

Muslim scholars have different opinions on this matter. For instance, Imam Maturidi and his school argue that no people can be excused, for there is enough evidence pointing to the One Creator to guide anyone to belief in Him. The 'Ashari school, referring to the above verse, argues that warning and guidance must precede judgment, and that people can be held responsible only if they have been sent a Prophet.

Others combine these two positions: Those who have not been sent a Prophet and so did not enter willfully into unbelief or idolatry are *ahl al-najat* (people who will be excused and so escape punishment and who, as God wills, may be saved). This position is based on the fact that some people cannot analyze their surroundings, penetrate to their meaning, or deduce the right course of belief and action. They first have to be taught the right way, given explanations and directions on how to act, and then they can be rewarded or punished according to what they do with the new knowledge. Those who willfully enter unbelief, fight belief and religion, or knowingly defy God and His commandments will be questioned and punished, regardless of how isolated they are.

How many Prophets were there? Were they all from Arabia?

Prophets were raised and sent to their people in different lands and at different times. One *hadith* puts the number of Prophets at 124,000[51]; another mentions 224,000. Both versions, however, should be evaluated critically according to the science of hadith. The exact number is not important; rather, we should realize that no people has ever been deprived of its own Prophet: *There never was a people without a Warner having lived among them* (35:24) and: *We never punish until We have sent a Messenger* (17:15).

To punish a people before warning them that what they are doing is wrong is contrary to His Glory and Grace. The warning precedes responsibility, which may be followed by reward or punishment: *Anyone who has done an atom's weight of good shall see it. And anyone who has done an atom's weight of evil shall see it* (99:7-8). If a Prophet has not been sent, people cannot know what is right and wrong and so cannot be punished. However, since every individual will

---

[51] Ibn Hanbal, *Musnad*, 5:169.

be called to account for his or her good and evil deeds, we may infer that a Prophet has been sent to every people: *We sent among every people a messenger with (the command): "Serve God and avoid evil"* (16:36).

The Prophets were not raised only in Arabia. In fact, we do not even know all of the Prophets who were raised there, let alone elsewhere. We know only 28 of them by name (from Adam to Muhammad), and the Prophethood of three of them is uncertain.[52] We do not know exactly from where they emerged. Supposedly, Adam's tomb and the place of his re-union with Eve is Jidda, but this information is uncertain. We know that Abraham spent some time in Anatolia, Syria, and Babylon. Lot was associated with Sodom and Gomorrah, around the Dead Sea; Shu'ayb with Madyan; Moses with Egypt; and Yahya and Zakariyya with the Mediterranean countries—they may have crossed to Anatolia, since Christians link Mary (Maryam) and Jesus with Ephesus. But these associations remain suppositions at best.

We know the names of some Prophets sent to the Israelites, but not the names of any others or where they appeared. Moreover, because their teachings have been distorted and lost over time, we cannot say anything about who they were and where they were sent.

Take the case of Christianity. Following the Council of Nicea (325 CE), the original doctrine of God's Oneness was dropped in favor of the human-made doctrine of the Trinity. For the Catholic Church, Jesus became the "son" of God, while his mother Mary became the "mother" of God. Some believed, rather vaguely, that God was immanent or present in things. Thus, Christianity came to resemble the idolatrous

---

[52] Luqman (31:12), Uzayr (9:30), and Zul-qarnain (18:83-98).

beliefs and practices of ancient Greece, and its followers began to associate other things and people with God, a major sin in Islam.

Throughout history, deviations and corruption of the Truth started and increased in this way. If the Qur'an had not informed us of the Prophethood of Jesus and of the purity and greatness of Mary, we would have difficulty in distinguishing the cults of and rites of Jupiter (Zeus) and Jesus, Venus (Aphrodite) and Mary.

This same process may have happened to other religions. As such, we cannot say definitely that their founders or teachers were Prophets or that they taught in a specific location. We only can speculate that Confucius, Buddha, or even Socrates were Prophets. We cannot give a definite answer because we do not have enough information about them and their original teachings. However, we know that the teachings of Confucius and Buddha influenced great numbers of their contemporaries and continue to do so.

Some say that Socrates was a philosopher influenced by Judaism, but they offer no proof. Words attributed to him by Plato imply that Socrates was "inspired" from a very early age to "instruct" people in true understanding and belief. But it is not clear if these words are attributed correctly or exactly what his people understood them to mean. Only this much is reliable: Socrates taught in an environment and manner that supports the use of reason.

Professor Mahmud Mustafa's observations of two primitive African tribes confirm what has been said above. He remarks that the Maw-Maws believe in God and call him Mucay. This God is one and only, acts alone, does not beget or is begotten, and has no associate or partner. He is not seen or sensed, but known only through His works. He dwells in the heavens, from where he ordains everything. That is why the Maw-Maws raise their hands when praying. Another tribe, the Neyam-Neyam, expresses similar themes. There is one God who decrees and ordains everything, and what he says is absolute. He makes everything in the forest move according to His will, and sends thunderbolts against those with whom he is angry.

These ideas are compatible with what is said by the Qur'an. The Maw-Maws's belief is very close to what we find in the Qur'an's *Surat al-Ikhlas*. How could these primitive tribes, so far removed from civilization and the known Prophets, have so pure and sound a concept of God? This reminds us of the Qur'anic verse: *For every people there is a messenger. When their messenger comes, the matter is judged between them with justice, and they are not wronged* (10:47).

Professor Adil of Kirkuk, Iraq, was working as a mathematician at Riyadh University when I met him in 1968. He told me that he had met many Native American Indians while earning his Ph.D. in the United States. He had been struck by how many of them believe in One God who does not eat or sleep or find himself constrained by time. He rules and governs all of creation, which is under His sovereignty and dependent on His will. They also referred to some of God's attributes: the lack of a partner, for such would surely give rise to conflict.

How does one reconcile the alleged primitiveness of such peoples with such loftiness in their concept of God? It seems that true Messengers conveyed these truths to them, some soundness of which can still be found in their present-day beliefs.

Some people wonder why there were no female Prophets. The overwhelming consensus of Sunni scholars of the Law and Tradition is that no woman has been sent as Prophet. Except for a questionable and even unreliable tradition that Mary and Pharaoh's wife were sincere believers, there is no Qur'anic authority or *hadith* that a woman was sent to her people as a Prophet.

God the All-Mighty created all entities in pairs. Humanity was created to be the steward of creation, and thus is fitted to it. The pairs of male and female are characterized by complex relation of mutual attraction and repulsion. Women incline toward softness, weakness, and compassion; men incline toward strength, force, and competitive toughness. When they come together, such characteristics allow them to establish a harmonious family unit.

Today, the issue of gender has reached the point where some people refuse to recognize the very real differences between men and women and claim that they are alike and equal in all respects. Implementing these views has resulted in the "modern" lifestyle of women working outside the home, trying to "become men," and thus losing their own identity. Family life has eroded, for children are sent to day-care centers or boarding schools as parents are too busy, as "individuals," to take proper care of them. This violence against nature and culture has destroyed the home as a place of balance between authority and love, as a focus of security and peace.

God the Wise ordained some principles and laws in the universe, and created human beings therein with an excellent and lofty nature. Men are physically stronger and more capable than women, and plainly constituted to strive and compete without needing to withdraw from the struggle. It is different with women, because of their menstrual period, their necessary confinement before and after childbirth, and their consequent inability to observe all the prayers and fasts. Nor can women be available continually for public duties. How could a mother with a baby in her lap lead and administer armies, make life and death decisions, and sustain and prosecute a difficult strategy against an enemy?[53]

A Prophet must lead humanity in every aspect of its social and religious life without a break. That is why Prophethood is impossible for women. If men could have children, they could not be Prophets either. Prophet Muhammad points to this fact when he describes women as "those who cannot fulfil the religious obligations totally and cannot realize some of them."[54]

A Prophet is an exemplar, a model for conducting every aspect of human life, so that people cannot claim that they were asked to do things that they could not do. Exclusively female matters are communicated to other women by the women in the Prophet's household.

Was Prophet Muhammad's mission limited and temporary?

All of the available information and resources, including his life, shows that his mission was universal and eternal.

Such men as Alexander the "Great," the Roman Caesars, Napoleon, Hitler, and the imperialists of Europe, Russia, and America all sought extensive dominion for the sake of worldly power and authority. But when Prophet Muhammad told

---

[53] Remember that we are talking about the past, not today, where circumstances have changed completely due to scientific advancements and modern conveniences. As there can be no more Prophets after Muhammad, this point is moot.

[54] Bukhari, *Hayd,* 6.

his followers to spread Islam all over the world, his aim was to remove the obstacles preventing human happiness in this world and the next, to prevent them from going to Hell, and to enable them to regain their lost values and inherent purity. As the final Messenger, always under His Guidance and Command, his life was a struggle to spread the light of Islam as far as possible so that others might hear the Divine Message. Certainly he succeeded.

Let's go over some points that demonstrate his mission's universality:

- While still in Makka, he sent some Muslims to Abyssinia. Through the efforts of those believers, many Abyssinians had the chance to know and embrace Islam. While this migration was undertaken to escape intense persecution at home, it also caused the king Negus and other Abyssinian nobles to convert to Islam. This was one of the first proofs of universality.

- Among the early Muslims were Bilal (from Abyssinia), Suhayb (from Rum [Byzantium]), Salman (from Persia), and others. Although they were from different nations and races, they were in the first rank of Muslims. Furthermore, the fact that such people and many more non-Arabs were given higher ranks and esteem than many Arabs shows that Islam, from the beginning, had a universal perspective.

- Long before the conquest of Iraq and Persia, the Prophet told Suraqa that one day he would wear the bracelets of Chosroes, son of Ormuz, Emperor of Persia.[55] This indicates that the Prophet knew that Islam would be carried to

---

[55] Before converting to Islam, Suraqa chased the Prophet during his emigration to Madina. *Al-Kamil*, 2:74.

Iraq and Persia, and implies that it had to be carried there. It happened just as the Prophet predicted.

• While resting in the house of Umm Haram bint Milhan (his paternal aunt and wife of 'Ubada ibn Samit), the Prophet slept for a short while. When he awoke, he said smilingly: My community has been shown to me. I saw it waging war on the seas like kings sitting on thrones." [56] Forty years later, Umm Haram accompanied 'Ubada on the conquest of Cyprus. She died and was buried there, where her grave can still be seen. As before, it was an indication from the Prophet that his Companions would, and must, carry the Divine Message overseas.

• Once the Prophet told his Companions: "Egypt will be conquered after my death. Be kind and benevolent to its people. Deal with them gently, for there is kinship and duty between you and them." [57] So he informed them that Islam would reach Egypt during their lifetimes, and asked them to preserve the kinship established by his marriage to Mary, the Egyptian Copt.[58]

---

[56] Al-Bidaya wa al-Nihaya, 7:152.

[57] Al-Tabari, 4:228.

[58] Copts belong to an autonomous Christian sect that has been based in Egypt since the earliest days of Christianity. They adhere to Monophysitism. According to www.encyclopedia.com, Monophysitism is "a heresy of the 5th and 6th cent., a reaction against Nestorianism. It challenged the orthodox creed of the Council of Chalcedon (451) by saying Jesus had only a divine nature. For invalidating Chalcedon, the East was put under excommunication by the pope until 519. In Syria, Egypt, and Armenia, Monophysitism dominated, and a permanent schism set in by 600, resulting in the creation of the Jacobite, Coptic, and Armenian churches."

- Before the Battle of Khandaq, while he was digging the ditch, the Prophet foretold the conquest of Hira, the fall of the columns of Chosroes' palace (the Persian Empire), and the capture of Damascus. It happened as he foretold.[59]

Many Prophetic traditions and Qur'anic verses also state clearly that his Prophethood was for all nations and all times. Among them are the following:

- In one hadith, the Prophet says: "Each Messenger was sent to his own nation. I was sent to humanity."[60] In another tradition, it is narrated as "to blacks and whites." Confirming this, al-Tabari narrates a different hadith: "I was sent to all both as a mercy and a Prophet. Complete my mission. May God's mercy be on you."[61]

- When Chosroes' envoy visited him, the Prophet said to him: "In the near future, my religion and its sovereignty will reach Chosroes' throne."[62]

- Centuries before the conquest of Anatolia and Constantinople (now Istanbul), he foretold that Muslim armies would reach Europe and that Constantinople would be conquered. Many attempts were made to realize this and be blessed, for, in the words of the Prophet: "Constantinople will be conquered. Blessed is the commander who will conquer it, and blessed are his troops."[63] Since

---

[59] *Al-Bidaya wa al-Nihaya*, 4:99.

[60] Bukhari, *Jihad*, 122.

[61] Al-Tabari, 2:625.

[62] *Al-Kamil*, 2:146.

[63] Ibn Hanbal, *Musnad*, 4:335.

that city was a symbol of a large dominion, the Prophet was directing his community to carry Islam worldwide.

The Qur'anic verses related to the Prophet's mission are all self-explanatory. They say unmistakably that the Divine Revelation, through the Prophet, was meant for all humanity. Muhammad was commissioned to warn both humanity and jinn. For instance:

> This is no less than a message to (all) the worlds (38:87).

> This is but a warning; an eloquent Qur'an to admonish the living and to pass judgment on the unbelievers (36:70).

> We have sent you to all humanity, giving them glad tidings and warning them, but most people understand not (34:28).

> Say: "O People! I am sent unto you all, as the Messenger, to whom belongs the dominion of the heavens and the Earth. (7:158)

The Qur'an states that former Prophets were sent to their particular community or nation, and draws our attention to the difference between them and Prophet Muhammad:

> We sent Noah to his people. He said: "O my people! Worship God! You have no other God but Him." (7:59)

> To the 'Ad, We sent Hud, one of their own brethren. He said: "O my people! Worship God! You have no other god but Him." (7:65)

> To the Thamud, We sent Salih, one of their own brethren. He said: "O my people! Worship God! You have no other god but Him." (7:73)

> We also sent Lut; He said to his people. (7:80)

> To the people of Madyan We sent Shu'ayb, one of their own brethren. (7:85)

Moreover, with almost every mention of these Prophets, the Qur'an states that they were raised from among their own brethren and sent to their own nation. Thus, there is no ambiguity over who was a Prophet for his own nation and who was the one for humanity.

Since the first revelation, the Prophet has been heard and respected almost everywhere. His teachings, which have established a way of life for peoples as far apart as China and Morocco, have touched the hearts of countless people in every part of the world. They have been—and remain—the most enduring model for a balanced, civilized life, and have led to human development in every field.

Despite the most vicious and sustained oppression of Muslims, the vandalizing of their culture, the misrepresentation of their values and history, Islam's principles and ideals remain fresh and vivid in the hearts of the great majority of Muslims. Indeed, true Muslims are respected, and even many non-Muslims agree that our problems can be resolved only by applying those principles. Islam's sheer endurance, through the conquest and defeat of its followers as well as among so many different peoples and languages, cultures, and climates, proves that Prophet Muhammad's mission is for all people and eternal.

Why was the Prophet polygamous?

Some critics of Islam have reviled the Prophet as a self-indulgent libertine. They have accused him of character failings that are hardly compatible with being of average virtue, let alone with being a Prophet and God's last Messenger, as well as the best model for humanity to follow. However, based on the easily available scores of biographies and well-authenticated accounts of his sayings and actions, it is quite clear that he lived the most strictly disciplined life, and that his marriages were part of the numerous burdens he bore as God's last Messenger.

The reasons for his multiple marriages vary. However, all of them were related to his role as leader of the Muslim community, and his responsibility to guide the new Muslims toward the norms and values of Islam.

When Muhammad was 25, before he was called to his future mission, he married Khadija, his first wife. Given the surrounding cultural environment, not to mention the climate and such other considerations as his youth, it is remarkable that he enjoyed a reputation for perfect chastity, integrity, and trustworthiness. As soon as he was called to Prophethood, he acquired enemies who did not hesitate to raise false calumnies against him—but not once did any of them dare invent something unbelievable about him.

Khadija was 15 years his senior. This marriage was very high and exceptional in the eyes of the Prophet and God. For 23 years, their life was a period of uninterrupted contentment in perfect fidelity. In the eighth year of Prophethood, however, she passed away, leaving the Prophet as the sole parent of their children for 4 or 5 years. Even his enemies are forced to admit that, during these years, they can find no flaw in his moral character. The Prophet took no other wife during Khadija's lifetime, although public opinion would have allowed him to do so. When he began marrying other women, he was already past 55, when very little real interest and desire for marriage remains.[64]

---

[64] Keep in mind that we must judge the Prophet's actions by the standards of his own time. Lifespans were short, so at 55 he was already considered quite old. Obviously, this has changed somewhat in our own time, due to scientific and medical advances.

How could a Prophet by polygamous? This question is often asked by people without any religion, or by Jews and Christians. In respect to the first group, they have no right to reproach people who follow a religious way of life. Their own conduct with the opposite sex follows nothing but their own desire, regardless of what they say. They do not worry about the consequences of such liaisons to themselves, to the resulting children, or how their loose behavior impacts young people in general. Viewing themselves as free, they engage in such condemned practices as homosexuality and, even more extreme (but hopefully limited), incest, pedophilia, and multiple male/female partners (meaning that the child's true father is unknown). Such people criticize the Prophet only to drag others down to their own level.

Jews and Christians who attack the Prophet for his polygamy do so out of their fear and jealous hatred of Islam. They forget that the great Jewish patriarchs, called Prophets in the Bible and the Qur'an and revered by the followers of all three faiths as exemplars of moral excellence, all practiced polygamy on a far greater scale.[65]

Polygamy did not originate with the Muslims. Furthermore, in the case of the Prophet this practice has far more significance than people generally realize. In a sense, the Prophet had to be polygamous to transmit his Sunna (the statutes and norms of Islamic law). As Islam covers every part of one's life, private spousal relations cannot remain untouched. Therefore, there must be women who can guide other women in these matters. There is no room for the allusive language of hints and innuendoes. The chaste and virtuous women of the Prophet's household were responsible for

---

[65] According to I Kings 11:3, Solomon had *700 wives, princesses, and 300 concubines.*

explaining the norms and rules of such private spheres to other Muslims.

Some of the Prophet's marriages were contracted for specific reasons:

- Since his wives were young, middle-aged, and old, the requirements and norms of Islamic law could be exemplified in relation to their different life stages and experiences. These were learned and applied first within the Prophet's household, and then passed on to other Muslims by his wives.

- Each wife was from a different clan or tribe, which allowed the Prophet to establish bonds of kinship and affinity throughout the rapidly expanding Muslim community. This also enabled a profound attachment to him to spread among all Muslims, thereby creating and securing equality and brotherhood in a most practical way and on the basis of religion.

- Each wife, both during and after the Prophet's life, proved to be of great benefit and service to the cause of Islam. They conveyed his message and interpreted it to their clans: the outer and inward experience, and the qualities, manners, and faith of the man whose life was the embodiment of the Qur'an—Islam in practice. In this way, all Muslims learned about the Qur'an, *hadith,* Qur'anic interpretation and commentary, and Islamic jurisprudence, and so became fully aware of Islam's essence and spirit.

- Through his marriages, the Prophet established ties of kinship throughout Arabia. This gave him the freedom to move and be accepted as a member in each family. Since they regarded him as one of their own, they felt they could go to him in person and ask him directly about this life and the Hereafter. The tribes also benefited collectively from their proximity to him: they considered themselves fortunate and took pride in that relationship, such as the Umayyads (through Umm Habiba), the Hashimites (through Zaynab bint Jahsh), and the Bani Makhzum (through Umm Salama).

What we have said so far is general and could, in some respects, be true of all Prophets. However, now we will discuss the life sketches of *Ummahat al-Mu'minin* (the mothers of the believers), not in the order of the marriages but from a different perspective.

Khadija was the Prophet's first wife. As mentioned above, she married him before his call to Prophethood. Even though she was 15 years his senior, she bore all of his children, except for Ibrahim, who did not survive infancy. Khadija was also his friend, the sharer of his inclinations and ideals to a remarkable degree. Their marriage was wonderfully blessed, for they lived together in profound harmony for 23 years. Through every trial and persecution launched by the Makkan unbelievers, she was his dearest companion and helper. He loved her very deeply and married no other woman while she was alive.

This marriage is the ideal of intimacy, friendship, mutual respect, support, and consolation. Though faithful and loyal to all his wives, he never forgot Khadija and mentioned her virtues and merits extensively on many occasions. He married another woman only 4 or 5 years after Khadija's death. Until that time, he served as both a mother and a father to his children, providing their daily food and provisions as well as bearing their troubles and hardships. To allege that such a man was a sensualist or driven by sexual lust is nonsensical.

'**A'isha** was the daughter of Abu Bakr, his closest friend and devoted follower. One of the earliest converts, Abu Bakr had long hoped to cement the deep attachment between himself and the Prophet through marriage. By marrying 'A'isha, the Prophet accorded the highest honor and courtesy to a man who had shared all the good and bad times with him. In this way, Abu Bakr and 'A'isha acquired the distinction of being spiritually and physically close to the Prophet.

'A'isha proved to be a remarkably intelligent and wise woman, for she had both the nature and temperament to carry forward the work of Prophetic mission. Her marriage prepared her to be a spiritual guide and teacher to all women. She became one of the Prophet's major students and disciples. Through him, like so many Muslims of that blessed time, her skills and talents were matured and perfected so that she could join him in the abode of bliss both as wife and as student.

Her life and service to Islam prove that such an exceptional person was worthy to be the Prophet's wife. She was one of the greatest authorities on hadith, an excellent Qur'anic commentator, and a most distinguished and knowledgeable expert on Islamic law. She truly represented the inner and outer qualities and experiences of Prophet Muhammad. This is surely why the Prophet was told in a dream that he would marry 'A'isha. Thus, when she was still innocent and knew nothing of men and worldly affairs, she was prepared and entered the Prophet's household.

Umm Salama, of the Makhzum clan, was first married to her cousin. The couple had embraced Islam at the very beginning and emigrated to Abyssinia to avoid persecution. After their return, they and their four children migrated to Madina. Her husband participated in many battles and died after being severely wounded at the Battle of Uhud. Abu Bakr and 'Umar proposed marriage to her, aware of her needs and suffering as a destitute widow with children to support. She refused, believing that no one could be better than her late husband.

Some time after that, the Prophet proposed marriage. This was quite right and natural, for this great woman had never shied from sacrifice and suffering for Islam. Now that she was alone after having lived many years in the noblest Arabian clan, she could not be neglected and left to beg her way in life. Considering her piety, sincerity, and what she had suffered, she certainly deserved to be helped. By marrying her, the Prophet was doing what he had always done: befriending those lacking in friends, supporting the unsupported, and protecting the unprotected. In her present circumstances, there was no kinder or more gracious way of helping her.

Umm Salama also was intelligent and quick to understand. She had all the capacities and gifts to become a spiritual guide and teacher. When the Prophet took her under his protection, a new student to whom all women would be grateful was accepted into the school of knowledge and guidance. As the Prophet was now almost 60, marrying a widow with many children and assuming the related expenses and responsibilities can only be understood as an act of compassion that deserves our admiration for his infinite reserves of humanity.

Umm Habiba was the daughter of Abu Sufyan, an early and most determined enemy of the Prophet and supporter of Makkah's polytheistic and idolatrous religion. Yet his daughter was one of the earliest Muslims. She emigrated to Abyssinia with her husband, where he eventually renounced his faith and embraced Christianity. Although separated from her husband,[66] she remained a Muslim. Shortly after that, her husband died and she was left all alone and desperate in exile.

The Companions, at that time few in number and barely able to support themselves, could not offer much help. So, what were her options? She could convert to Christianity and get help that way (unthinkable). She could return to her father's home, now a headquarters of the war against Islam (unthinkable). She could wander from house to house as a beggar, but again it was an unthinkable option for a member of one of the richest and noblest Arab families to bring shame upon her family name by doing so.

God recompensed Umm Habiba for her lonely exile in an insecure environment among people of a different race and religion, and for her despair at her husband's apostasy and death, by arranging for the Prophet to marry her. Learning of her plight, the Prophet sent an offer of marriage through the king Negus. This noble and generous action was a practical proof of: *We have not sent you save as a mercy for all creatures* (21:107).

Thus Umm Habiba joined the Prophet's household as a wife and student, and contributed much to the moral and spiritual life of those who learned from her. This marriage linked Abu Sufyan's powerful family to the Prophet's person and household, which caused its members to re-evaluate their attitudes. It also is correct to trace the influence of this marriage, beyond the family of Abu Sufyan and to the Umayyads in general, who ruled the Muslims for almost a century.

---

[66] Muslim women are not allowed to marry non-Muslim men. This is because the man is regarded as responsible for his wife and out of concern for the children's spiritual well-being.

This clan, whose members had been the most fanatical in their hatred of Islam, produced some of Islam's most renowned early warriors, administrators, and governors. Without doubt, it was this marriage that began this change, for the Prophet's depth of generosity and magnanimity of soul surely overwhelmed them.

Zaynab bint Jahsh was a lady of noble birth and a close relative of the Prophet. She was, moreover, a woman of great piety, who fasted much, kept long vigils, and gave generously to the poor. When the Prophet arranged for her to marry Zayd, an African ex-slave whom he had adopted as his son, Zaynab's family and Zaynab herself were at first unwilling. The family had hoped to marry their daughter to the Prophet. But when they realized that the Prophet had decided otherwise, they consented out of deference to their love for the Prophet and his authority.

Zayd had been enslaved as a child during a tribal war. Khadija, who had bought him, had given him to Muhammad as a present when she married him. The Prophet had freed immediately him and, shortly afterwards, adopted him as his son. He insisted on this marriage to establish and fortify equality between the Muslims, and to break down the Arab prejudice against a slave or even freedman marrying a free-born woman.

The marriage was an unhappy one. The noble-born Zaynab was a good Muslim of a most pious and exceptional quality. The freedman Zayd was among the first to embrace Islam, and he also was a good Muslim. Both loved and obeyed the Prophet, but they were not a compatible couple. Zayd asked the Prophet several times to allow them to divorce. However, he was told to persevere with patience and not separate from Zaynab.

But then one day Gabriel came with a Divine Revelation that the Prophet's marriage to Zaynab was a bond already contracted: *We have married her to you* (33:37).[67] This command was one of the severest trials the Prophet, had yet had to face, for he was being told to break a social taboo. Yet it had to be done for the sake of God, just as God commanded. 'A'isha later said: "Had the Messenger been inclined to suppress any part of the Revelation, surely he would have suppressed this verse." [68]

Divine wisdom decreed that Zaynab join the Prophet's household, so that she could be prepared to guide and enlighten the Muslims. As his wife, she proved herself most worthy of her new position by always being aware of her responsibilities and the courtesies proper to her role, all of which she fulfilled to universal admiration.

Before Islam, an adopted son was considered a natural son. Therefore, an adopted son's wife was considered as a natural son's wife would be. According to the Qur'anic verse, former "wives of your sons proceeding from your loins" fall within the prohibited degrees of marriage. But this prohibition does not apply to adopted sons, for there is no real consanguinity. What now seems obvious was not so then. This deeply rooted tribal taboo was broken by this marriage, just as God had intended.

To have an unassailable authority for future generations of Muslims, the Prophet had to break this taboo himself. It is one more instance of his deep faith that he did as he was told, and freed his people from a legal fiction that obscured a biological, natural reality.

---

[67] Bukhari, *Tawhid,* 22.

[68] Bukhari and Muslim.

Juwayriya bint Harith, the daughter of Harith, chief of the defeated Bani Mustaliq clan, was captured during a military campaign. She was held with other members of her proud family alongside her clan's "common" people. She was in great distress when she was taken to the Prophet, for her kinsmen had lost everything and she felt profound hate and enmity for the Muslims. The Prophet understood her wounded pride, dignity, and suffering; more important, he understood how to deal with these issues effectively. He agreed to pay her ransom, set her free, and offered to marry her.

When the Ansar and the Muhajirun realized that the Bani Mustaliq now were related to the Prophet by marriage, they freed about 100 families that had not yet been ransomed.[69] A tribe so honored could not be allowed to remain in slavery. In this way, the hearts of Juwayriya and her people were won. Those 100 families blessed the marriage. Through his compassionate wisdom and generosity, the Prophet turned a defeat for some into a victory for all, and what had been an occasion of enmity and distress became one of friendship and joy.

Safiyya bint Huyayy was the daughter of the chief of the Jewish tribe of Khaybar, who had persuaded the Bani Qurayza to break their treaty with the Prophet. From her earliest days, she had seen her family and relatives oppose the Prophet. She had lost her father, brother, and husband in battles against the Muslims, and eventually was captured by them.

The attitudes and actions of her family and relatives might have nurtured in her a deep desire for revenge. However, 3

---

[69] The Ansar (the Helpers) were the Muslims of Madina who welcomed the Muhajirun (the Prophet's Makkan followers) into their town, accepted the Prophet as their leader, and took care of them. Ibn Hanbal, *Musnad*, 6:277.

days before the Prophet reached Khaybar, she dreamed of a brilliant moon coming out from Madina, moving toward Khaybar, and falling into her lap. She later said: "When I was captured, I began to hope that my dream would come true." When she was brought before the Prophet as a captive, he set her free and offered her the choice of remaining a Jewess and returning to her people, or entering Islam and becoming his wife. "I chose God and his Messenger," she said. Shortly after that, they were married.

Elevated to the Prophet's household, she witnessed at first hand the Muslims' refinement and true courtesy. Her attitude to her past experiences changed, and she came to appreciate the great honor of being the Prophet's wife. As a result of this marriage, the attitude of many Jews changed as they came to see and know the Prophet closely. It is worth noting that such close relations between Muslims and non-Muslims can help people to understand each other better and to establish mutual respect and tolerance as social norms.

Sawda bint Zam'ah ibn Qays was the widow of Sakran. Among the first to embrace Islam, they had emigrated to Abyssinia to escape the Makkans' persecution. Sakran died in exile, and left his wife utterly destitute. As the only means of assisting her, the Prophet, though himself having a hard time making ends meet, married her. This marriage took place some time after Khadija's death.

Hafsa was the daughter of 'Umar ibn al-Khattab. She had lost her husband, who emigrated to both Abyssinia and Madina, where he was fatally wounded in the path of God. She remained widowed for a while. 'Umar desired the honor and blessing of being close to the Prophet in this world and in the Hereafter. The Prophet honored this by marrying Hafsa to protect and to help the daughter of his faithful disciple.

Given the above facts, it is clear that the Prophet married these women for a variety of reasons: to provide helpless or widowed women with dignified subsistence; to console and honor enraged or estranged tribes; to bring former enemies into some degree of relationship and harmony; to gain certain uniquely gifted men and women for Islam; to establish new norms of relationship between people within the unifying brotherhood of faith in God; and to honor with family bonds the two men who were to be the first leaders of the Muslim community after his death. These marriages had nothing to do with self-indulgence, personal desire, or lust. With the exception of 'A'isha, all of the Prophet's wives were widows, and all of his post-Khadija marriages were contracted when he was already an old man. Far from being acts of self-indulgence, these marriages were acts of self-discipline.

Part of that discipline was providing each wife with the most meticulously observed justice, dividing equally whatever slender resources he allowed for their subsistence, accommodation, and allowance. He also divided his time with them equally, and regarded and treated them with equal friendship and respect. The fact that all of his wives got on well with each other is no small tribute to his genius for creating peace and harmony. With each of them, he was not only a provider but also a friend and companion.

The number of the Prophet's wives was a dispensation unique to him. Some of the merits and wisdom of this dispensation, as we understand them, have been explained. All other Muslims are allowed a maximum of four wives at one time. When that Revelation restricting polygamy came, the Prophet's marriages had already been contracted. Thereafter, he married no other women.

CHAPTER 5

Satan

What is Satan is and why was he created?

Satan was created from fire, like the jinn with whom he mostly kept company. Before his obedience and sincerity was tested through Adam, he had been in the company of angels, acting and worshipping as they did. Unlike angels who follow orders and never rebel against God (66:6), Satan can choose his own path of conduct.[70] When God tested him together with the angels by commanding them to prostrate before Adam (i.e., humanity), the seeds of self-conceit and disobedience in his nature burst open and swallowed him: *I am better than him. You created me from fire, whilst him you did create of clay* (38.76).

Satan was created for important purposes. First of all, if Satan did try continually to seduce humanity, our creation would have been meaningless and futile. God has innumerable servants who cannot rebel and therefore do whatever they are commanded. In fact, the existence of an absolute Divine Being Who has many beautiful Names and Attributes requires, not by way of external necessity but due to the essential nature of His Names, that His Names be

---

[70] Known as Iblis before refusing God's command to prostrate before Adam, he has limited free will.

manifest.[71] He manifests all of His Names only through humanity.

Since He has free will, He gave us free will, by which is meant the ability to choose between alternatives. In addition, God endowed us with great potentials. The purpose of the constant inner and outer struggles that we face is the direct result of our ability to choose and to develop those potentials. Just as God sends hawks upon sparrows so that the latter can develop their potential to escape, He created Satan and allowed him to tempt us so that we can rise to higher spiritual ranks and strengthen our willpower by resisting temptation. As hunger stimulates people and animals to further exertion and discovery of new ways to be satisfied, and fear inspires new ways of defense, Satan's temptations cause us to develop our potentials and to be alert against sin.

Angels do not rise to the higher spiritual ranks, for Satan cannot tempt them or lead them astray. Animals have fixed stations, meaning that they can neither ascend or descend. Only humanity is faced with an infinite number of ranks or stations, and only we can rise or fall accordingly. There is an infinitely long line of spiritual evolution between the ranks of the greatest Prophets and saints down to such people as Pharaoh and Nimrod.

Given this, we cannot claimed that the creation of Satan is an evil. Although Satan is an evil creature, God's creation involves the whole universe and should be understood in relation to the results, not only with respect to the acts themselves. Whatever God does or creates is good and beautiful either in itself or in its effects. For example, rain and fire pro-

---

[71] Such as the Creator, the All-Merciful, the All-Providing, the All-Living and Giver of Life, the All-Beautiful, and the All-Powerful, among others.

duce many effects, almost all of which are useful. If some people are harmed by water and fire through their own abuse of them, we cannot claim that their creation is not wholly good. Similarly, the main purpose for creating Satan is to enable us to develop our potentials, strengthen our willpower by resisting temptation, and to rise to higher spiritual ranks.

Some argue that many people fall into unbelief and so enter Hell because of Satan's temptations. To such people, I respond: Although Satan was created for many good and universal purposes, people can be deceived by him. However, Satan cannot compel us to commit a wrong or a sin; his power is limited to that of suggestion and encouragement. If we are so weak that we allow Satan to deceive us and thus follow him, it is our own fault that we end up in Hell.

This is a suitable punishment for our misuse of an important faculty on which God conferred existence so that we can develop our potentials and achieve high spiritual ranks. Our task is to use our free will, which largely makes us human and allows us to have the highest position in creation, in the cause of intellectual and spiritual evolution. If we do not do so, it means that we complain of being honored with free will and of our own humanity.

Second, quality is far more important than quantity. Given this, we should consider qualitative (instead of quantitative) values when judging. For example, 100 date pits are worth only 100 cents as long as they remain as seeds. Their value can increase only if they are planted and grow into palm trees. But if only 20 actually grow into palm trees, can we say that it is "evil" to plant and water them? Clearly, it is wholly good to have 20 trees in exchange for 20 puts, since 20 trees will give 20,000 pits.

Again, say that 100 peahen eggs are worth 500 cents. But if only 20 eggs produce chicks, who would consider it an evil to risk producing 20 chicks at the expense of the other 80 eggs? On the contrary, it is wholly good to have 20 birds at the expense of 80 eggs, worth 400 cents, because those 20 chicks will be worth far more money, and some will even lay eggs.

The same is true with humanity. By resisting Satan and our evil-commanding selves, humanity has gained thousands of Prophets, countless saints and people of wisdom, knowledge, sincerity, and good morals. All of these people are the sun, moon, and stars of the human world. In exchange for such people, far more lower-quality people were lost.

What about involuntary thoughts and fancies?

Involuntary evil thoughts, fancies, or associations of ideas usually are the result of Satan's whispering. Just as a battery has two poles, so do our hearts have two central points or poles.[72] Like the two poles of a battery, there are two central points or poles in man's heart: One receives angelic inspiration, and the other is vulnerable to Satan's whispering.

Satan attacks those believers who are trying to deepen their belief and devotion. If they are scrupulous and delicate in feeling, he attacks them from different directions. When confronted with unbelievers, who follow him voluntarily by indulging in passing fancies and bodily pleasures, he whispers to them new and original ideas. In this way, he encourages them to increase their unbelief and learn new ways of struggling against true religion and all believers.

---

[72] By "heart" we mean the seat or center of spiritual intellect.

Satan's attacks from different directions. When God cursed Satan because of his haughty disobedience, Satan asked for respite until the Day of Judgment and permission to try to seduce human beings. God granted his request, and Satan retorted: *Then I shall come upon them from before them and from behind them and from their right and from their left, and you will not find most of them grateful* (7:17).

Satan does everything he can to seduce us. We are very complex beings, for God manifests all of His Names on us in this world of testing. We are sent here to be trained so that we can serve as a mirror to God and earn eternal happiness. In order to do this, we must train and develop all of our God-given feelings, faculties, and potentials. If some of these are not trained (e.g., intellect, anger, greed, obstinacy, and lust) and directed to lofty goals, but abused and used for disagreeable purposes, we will place our present and future life in danger. This is also true if we do not restrict our natural desires and animal by satisfying them in acceptable ways.

Approaching us from our left, Satan uses our animal aspect's feelings and faculties to tempt us into sin. When he approaches us from the front, he drives us to despair over our future, whispers that the Day of Judgment will never come, that whatever religions say about the Hereafter is mere fiction, and that religion belongs to the past and so is irrelevant to our present and future. When he comes upon us from behind, he tries to make us deny Prophethood, God's Existence and Unity, Divine Scriptures, angels, and other essential matters of belief. Through such whispers and suggestions, Satan tries to sever our connections with religion and steer us toward sin.

Satan cannot seduce devout, practicing believers in these ways. Rather, he approaches from the believer's right and encourages him to display and ostentation, to taking pride in their virtues and good deeds. He whispers that they are such good believers, until the believers' feelings of self-conceit and desire for praise are aroused. When this point is reached, believers begin to travel the road to perdition. For example, if we pray the supererogatory late night prayer and then proclaim it so that others will praise us, and if we begin to take credit for our accomplishments and good deeds while criticizing others behind their backs, it means that we have fallen under Satan's influence. We must do our best to resist Satan when he comes upon us from this direction.

Another of Satan's ruses is to make unimportant things seem important and vice versa. If believers dispute with each other over a secondary matter (e.g., using a rosary when glorifying God after the daily prescribed prayers) while their children are being dragged along ways of unbelief and materialism, or are drowning in the swamp of immorality, this indicates that Satan has seduced them.

Satan's whispering disagreeable thoughts and fancies. If Satan fails to seduce devout believers, he whispers some disagreeable thoughts and fancies to them. For example, through the association of ideas, he pushes believers toward having some negative conceptions of the Divine Being or of thinking about unbelief or disobedience. If we dwell on such thoughts, Satan pesters us until we fall into doubt about our belief or despair of a virtuous life.

Another ruse is to cause good, devout believers to suspect the correctness or validity of their religious acts. For example: Did I pray perfectly? Did I wash my face and hands completely while making *wudu'*? Have I washed the specific bodily parts the required number of times? Believers pestered with such involuntary thoughts, fancies, and doubts should know that their hearts have no part in them. Just as thieves attempt to rob rich people and strong countries try to control rich countries, so does Satan make a last-ditch effort to seduce believers by troubling their hearts.

This is similar to a sick person having a high temperature. We know that antibodies formed in a patient's blood to inhibit or destroy harmful bacteria or germs. This causes the body's temperature to rise. Similarly, a heart troubled with Satan's evil suggestions defends itself by fighting against them. Thus, the heart does not generate such thoughts, and neither does it approve of or adopt them. A reflection of something foul is not itself foul and cannot make us foul. In the same way, thinking about unbelief is not the same thing as actual unbelief.

We might even say that Satan's evil suggestions actually benefit believers, for they cause us to remain alert, to struggle against our carnal selves and Satan, and to progress toward ever-higher spiritual ranks.

How can we keep free of Satanic suggestions?

In fact, *the guile of Satan is ever feeble* (4:76). It is like a cobweb appearing before you—it cannot prevent you from going forward, and you do not have to attach any great importance to it. Satan only suggests or whispers, gilds sinful acts and presents them in falsely ornamented wrappers. Believers must never accept his invitations. When Satan resorts to whispering, we should realize that he is using his weakest strategy and ignore him. If we pay attention to these whisperings, we may be defeated. Like a commander whose fear causes him to hallucinate and then dispatch his soldiers to the wings, thereby leaving the center exposed, believers who listen to Satan weaken their ability to resist both him and their carnal selves. In the end, such believers are defeated.

Believers who want to avoid this trap should remain far away from sins, all of which Satan tries to make attractive. Heedlessness and neglect of worship are invitations to Satan's "arrows": *If anyone withdraws himself (or herself) from remembrance of the All-Merciful, We assign unto him (or her) a devil as a comrade* (43:36).

Remembering the All-Merciful, thinking about noble or sacred phenomena, and living a religious life protect us from Satan's attacks: *If a suggestion from Satan occurs to you, then seek refuge in God. He is All-Hearing, All-Knowing. Those who fear God and ward off (evil), when a passing notion from Satan troubles them, they remember, and behold, they see* (7:200-1).

The Messenger advised: "If you become angry while standing, sit down; if you are sitting, lie down or stand up and do *wudu'*." Once while returning from a military expedition, the Prophet called a halt at a certain place. They were so tired that they slept through the dawn prayer. When they woke up, the Prophet told them that they had to leave immediately, for "Satan rules here." The Prophet also says that Satan flees when the call to prayer is made.

Satan also uses obscene scenes to lead believers astray. He torments us with calls to illicit pleasures. On such occasions, we must remind ourselves that indulging in any illicit pleasure will engender remorse and may endanger both our present and future lives. We must never forget that the life of this world is but a passing plaything, a comforting illusion, and that the real or true life is that of the Hereafter. When some Companions hesitated to take part in the summer expedition to Tabuk because of the scorching heat, God warned them: *The heat of Hell is much more intense, if they would but understand* (9:81).

When Satan whispers evil thoughts, believers should realize that he is using his weakest strategy and that it can be ignored. Dwelling on such thoughts only exaggerates and aggravates our weakness or susceptibility. We also must avoid heedlessness and make sure that we do not neglect of worship, for such oversights attract Satan's attention. If we remember the All-Merciful, focus on noble or sacred phenomena and living a religious life, we will be able to resist Satan.

Why does Satan insist on his unbelief?

Shaytan, the Arabic word for Satan, means "being cast down from the Divine Presence, driven away in disgrace from God's mercy." Satan is like one who had all the trump cards but played them against himself, or like one who lost everything while on the verge of winning.

The Qur'an describes Satan's condition as follows:

> We created you and gave you shape; then We bade the angels to bow down to Adam, and they bowed down. Not so Iblis [Satan]; he refused to be of those who bow down. God asked: "Why didn't you bow down when I commanded you to do so?" He replied: "I am better than he. You created me from fire, and him from clay." (7:11-12)

Satan has gone so far astray that he cannot hear or realize the truth. He has become so perverse that he is the victim of his own vicious circle of depravity. In other words, he first victimized himself with his pride, vanity, and conceit. With his first satanic dialectic (I am better than he), he made his first tour of the vicious circle. He deprived himself of all the ways to beg pardon, and even to be forgiven, by making such excuses as: "I am better than he." Such a response clearly shows his conceit as well as his outpouring of pride, vanity, and arrogance.

Satan erred. So did Adam and Eve (Hawa') when they ate from the forbidden tree. However, as soon as they realized their mistake, Adam and Eve begged God to forgive them: *Our Lord! We have wronged our own souls: If you forgive us not and bestow not upon us Your mercy, we shall certainly be lost* (7:23). God granted their request, and so the vicious circle could not be established. Satan, on the other hand, attempted to justify himself and sought to prove his right and innocence by denying his mistake even after being warned about it. His continued insistence on being superior to Adam caused him to doom himself.

Many verses describe Satan's enmity, jealousy, and fight against humanity, as well as his impertinence, ignorance and disobedience toward God. Among them are the following: *Satan said: "Then by Your power, I will put them all in the wrong"* (28:82) and *I will lie in wait for them on your Straight Way. Then I will assault them, from their right, and their left. Nor will You find in most of them gratitude for Your mercies* (7:16-17).

Thus he became the archenemy of humanity. His error, self-defense, arrogance and rebellion resulted in his expulsion (7:13). This, along with his vow to corrupt people, removed him far away from the all-encompassing, enlightening, and elevating atmosphere of God's mercy. He indulged in and completely submitted himself to satanic logic, and chose the way of the most wicked seducer. The more he seduced, the more distant he became; the more distant he became, the more he felt malicious envy and rancor. This process caused him to acquire a second nature integrated with ingratitude, intrigue, malice and depravity.

As the distance grew, he became more vicious and corrupt. His rancor, vanity, and conceit increased. He dared to dispute with God, and removed himself even further His Mercy. His rebellion against and defiance of God sealed his doom: His heart was sealed. There now was nothing but evil in his heart, and any chance to do good or to reform himself was destroyed.

We are very honored beings. If we realize our full potential, we can become angelic. But we can also go in the other direction. Consider the following: Muslims who observe all of their religious duties and maintain excellent relations with others may, on occasion, lose their self-control and explode. At such times, they lose all their gentleness, compassion, pardon and tolerance. If you study them when they are in such a condition, you will see only hatred, malicious envy, rancor, and anger like the sparks of Hell. If you try to advise or counsel them at such times, you will not be able to get through to them.

Everyone has seen and experienced similar states. But we always retains the potential, through God's Mercy, of passing through such states and recovering virtue. By contrast, Satan is *permanently* in a state of hatred, malicious envy, and rancor. He can think only of evil and devilishness, for he no longer knows how to think of goodness. Although he knows God, Satan has forgotten compassion, gentleness and tolerance, all of which are mere obstacles to his self-conceit. In short, he worships his own selfhood. Our primary defense against falling into a similar state is to rely upon and believe in God. We resign ourselves to Him and depend on Him. May He save us from following Satan.

CHAPTER 6

Destiny and Free Will

> God lets go astray whoever He wills and guides aright
> whoever He wills (74:31).

Can we choose our actions?

Based on the verse cited above, it seems that God controls us. However, the Qur'an says that God has given us reason, intellect, and free will so that we can choose the way of good or evil. How can we reconcile these?

The Arabic word *hidaya* usually is translated as "guidance." However, it also has other meanings: rectitude, the straight way, the way to Islam, and the way of those upon whom God has bestowed His blessings. The Arabic word *dalala* usually is translated as "going astray." Among its other meanings are corruption, error, the way of those who persistently adhere to false beliefs and willfully break God's law, and those who refuse to listen to the truth and thus go astray out of their own heedlessness or negligence.

Being guided and being left astray relate to God and depend on His Will. He creates *hidaya* to manifest His Name *al-Hadi* (the One Who Guides) and *dalala* to manifest His Name *al-Mudil* (the One Who Leads Astray). He creates, or in other words, enables or "gives" being guided or being led astray. This does not mean that He leads someone on the right path or astray. Rather, being guided or being led astray result from our own intentions and actions, for such is a consequence of our attitudes and inclinations. It has nothing to do with an arbitrary predestination.

Guidance can be received by various actions: going to a mosque; listening to a sermon, a lecture, or the Qur'an; reflecting seriously on the Qur'an's verses and their meaning; spending time with pious people; receiving advice from sincere, spiritual guides and teachers of religion, and trying to benefit from their purity and lofty ethos; and reflecting on the true nature of life and death. Such practices lead to mental and spiritual enlightenment. If you start to do such things, no matter how apparently small or insignificant, God accepts it as a means to grant guidance. Therefore God guides, but the individual initiates the process. On the other hand, if you frequent such places as bars, nightclubs, or non-Islamic places of worship, in effect you are asking to be led astray. If God wills, He will let you go astray. If He does not, He will save you from such a destiny by any means He wishes.

Our share in determining whether we will be guided or go astray is infinitesimally small. If we follow misguidance, God creates the results from our own actions in accordance with the laws of cause and effect that He has decreed for His creation. It is a necessary condition of moral responsibility that we freely initiate actions that will lead us to misguidance if we choose to do so, despite all the warning and instruction we receive. Later on, God will punish or forgive us as He pleases.

Consider this example. When you listen to the Qur'an or a sermon, or read something about Islam, you experience certain feelings, a kind of inner uplifting and illumination. However, someone living next door to the mosque might consider the call to prayer, the sermons, and the prayers sources of irritation and complain that they are a public disturbance and nuisance. In either case, God uses our reactions and inclinations to create and enable the necessary results, wholly dependent on His Will, that may follow from that response.

Consider a different example. As we eat and drink, all kinds of nutrients, proteins, vitamins, carbohydrates, and so on are sent to where they are needed in our bodies. The mere wish or act of placing food in the mouth does not enable nourishment. First the faculties necessary to identify and move the food into the mouth, a complex coordination of brain and muscle activity, must be engaged and operative. No part of this process is controlled consciously or understood by the individual. Then, as the food enters the mouth, salivary glands begin to operate. Data about taste and flavor are passed to the brain, processed, and directed to the stomach, informing it of the precise combination of chemical substances necessary to digest that particular food and turn it into nourishment. And this is only the beginning!

As we have no conscious control over the process of nourishing our own body, we cannot say: "I put the food in my mouth, planned and arranged everything for the meal, digested it, distributed it to where it was needed, and fixed my body temperature for everything to function properly and efficiently. I did all this on my own!" If we did, would we not be ascribing to ourselves the actions of God? We should acknowledge reality: "When I put food in my mouth, wonderful processes begin to operate. An unseen, powerful hand puts these processes in motion for the necessary amount of time. The One who initiates and sustains all these processes is God."

By moving our will and inclination toward Divine Guidance, we may prove ourselves capable and worthy of it.

For instance: I long to talk about religion with fullness and ease, to express my heartfelt feelings so well that others may be moved and benefit—but I fail to achieve what I wish, and can do only so much. I wish to convey Qur'anic law and God's commandments through persuasive, sincere words— but I get stuck at some point and become tongue-tied. I long to be totally immersed in the rapture of prayer and to be rid of all worldly concerns while praying—but I can hardly manage one prayer out of a thousand in this way. In sum, I contribute a sincere wish or a will, even though I may not realize my goal. The realization of this belongs to the All-Mighty.

The love and pleasure of faith, the earnest desire for Heaven, and an inclination to be content and submissive in the face of whatever comes from God are gifts that only He can place in our hearts and souls. We choose and incline, and God accepts and bestows His Blessings and Guidance. Saduddin Taftazani said: "Faith is a flame that God lights in a person's soul as a consequence of his or her use of free will." In order to obtain so great a favor, we must use our free will. You press a button and your life is illuminated. This seemingly small effort of will, this inclining toward faith, becomes the means to acquire Guidance and to be illuminated by Divine Light.

Some people may ask: *If God lets go astray whomever He wills and guides aright whomever He wills* (74:31), how does He call His servants to account?

We cannot attribute evil to God, for that comes from ourselves: *Whatever good happens to you is from God; and whatever evil happens to you is from yourself* (4:79). We have only ourselves to blame for what we suffer, for *God does not wrong anyone as much as an atom's weight* (4:40). What happens to us is based upon our choices and actions, and accords with the law of cause and effect that God has decreed for His creation. Thus, those who persistently adhere to false beliefs and refuse to listen to and obey Divine commandments gradually lose the ability to perceive the truth, until a seal is set upon their hearts. Since God instituted these laws, sealing the heart and leading astray are attributed to Him. But in reality, such is the consequence of that person's free choice and inclination. Such a fate is neither predestined nor unjust.

Happiness in the Hereafter is the natural consequence of our effort to attain righteousness and inner illumination while alive: *None does He cause to go astray save the iniquitous, who break their bond with God after it has been established, and cut asunder what God has joined, and spread corruption on Earth* (2:26-27). God does not cause anyone to go astray, except those who He knows will refuse to seek faith. Here the causing to go astray denotes God's leaving the individual alone and removing His blessings. God may forsake one who He knows will choose to deny the truth and persevere in denial. Deserving His favor and blessings or deserving their withdrawal depend upon our free choice, and nothing else.

What happens to people born and living in non-Islamic countries?

Those who ask this question imply: "Since we believe in God and His Prophet, we will go to Paradise. But those who were born and live in non-Islamic countries do not benefit from the Divine Light and Guidance, so they will go to Hell." The question is a debating ploy, claiming on one the hand a greater concern for non-Muslims than that possessed by God and, on the other hand, sneaking in a criticism of Islam.

First, there is no general statement or decree in Islam that those who live in non-Islamic countries will go to Hell. Rather, the decree is this: If those who heard the Prophet's message and invitation, and witnessed the truth and light of Islam, reject it and turn away from it, they will go to Hell. Whether those who have heard the Divine Message live in Islamic countries is beside the point; what matters is that they heed and obey that Message. Those who do not do so will go to Hell—even if they were born and lived in Islamic countries.

Many Muslim scholars and theologians have spoken and written on what the Qur'an and the *hadith* say on the subject. But why do people dwell upon this sort of question? How will an answer affect or change their lives? Will it gain them anything in the Hereafter? Is there a difference between those who are willful unbelievers and those who do not believe because they have never heard of Islam? Will the latter go to Hell and suffer the same punishment?

The Ash'aris held that one who has not heard the name of God or the teachings of Islam will be "excused." God, as He wills, rewards such people for the good they have done, and they enjoy the blessings of Paradise.

The Maturidi view is somewhat similar to the Mu'tazili view. If such people find the Creator through the use of reason, even though they do not know His Names or Attributes, they will be saved. If they do not do this, they will not be saved. This position is not so different from that of the Ash'aris.

According to the Maturidis, it does not matter where one lives, for anyone can see the sun and moon rise and set, the stars sparkle, creation's balance and order, the splendor and regularity amid the enormous variety of creation, the grandeur of mountains and the gentle easing breezes on their slopes, and the thrilling colors and movements of flowers, trees, and animals. All of these are signs of the Owner,

Creator, Sustainer, and Administrator of all things. Therefore, people can observe and acknowledge the Creator's absolute existence, power, and grace without knowing His Names and Attributes, or His Books and Messengers. Such people are among the excused. That is why, when asked this question, we should refer to the view of the great imams of Islam.

Imam Ash'ari deduces his judgment from: *We never punish until We have sent a Messenger* (17:15). People cannot be punished for a wrong until due warning has reached them through a true Messenger.

According to the Maturidis, reason can distinguish good from evil. But it would be mistaken to say that reason can work everything out by itself. This is why God uses Messengers to relay His rulings of what is good and evil, and leaves nothing to fallible human judgment and experience. The Maturidi argument goes like this: Reason can work out that adultery and fornication are evil, because such practices interrupt genealogy and lineage and cause it to be lost, which, in turn, cause problems in inheritance and other matters. Reason can work out that theft is evil, for it allows no one to live in any degree of security; and that alcohol and other intoxicants are evil, because they cause people to lose consciousness, damage health, make them vulnerable to many illnesses, and can affect their offspring.

The same is true for what is good. Reason can grasp that faith in God is good, for it leads us to satisfaction and inner contentment. Even in this world, we begin to sense the contentment that we will have in Paradise. The way to faith is not so difficult. A bedouin once came to the Prophet and explained how he attained faith: "Camel droppings point to the existence of a camel. Footprints on the sand tell of a traveler. Heaven with its stars, the Earth with its mountains and valleys, and the sea with its waves—don't they point to the Maker, All-Powerful, Knowing, Wise, and Caring?" As he attained faith in God through his mind, we cannot underrate the role of reason and thinking in faith.

Setting out from this point, Maturidi says that one may find the Creator through reason. There are many examples from pre-Islamic times. One is Waraqa ibn Nawfal, Khadija's cousin, who felt that a Prophet would come during his lifetime because many of the signs had been fulfilled. When the first Revelation came to Muhammad, Khadija sought Waraqa's advice. He confirmed the truth of Muhammad's mission and revelations. Understanding that no good would ever come from the idols, Waraqa ignored them and, based on own judgment, believed in the existence of the One God.

Another such person was Zayd ibn 'Amr, 'Umar ibn al-Khattab's uncle. Knowing that the coming of a Prophet was imminent, he ignored the idols and worshipped the One God. Although he died before Muhammad's Prophethood, he intuitively knew it was coming. On his deathbed, he called his son Sa'id, 'Umar, and other family members and said: "The light of God is on the horizon. I believe it will emerge fully very soon. I already feel its signs over our heads. As soon as the Prophet comes, without losing any time, go and join him."

Any human-made "god" or "goddess" cannot be God or answer people's needs, for such things need those who created them. How can something that has needs and wants answer and provide for those who call upon it? Through such simple reasoning, we can realize our need to know the Lord of Heaven and Earth. When we direct our mind and reason to Revelation, our need to know is met and the way to eternal bliss is opened.

In sum, the only people who will go to Hell are those who see or hear about the Prophet and the Qur'an but do not seek further knowledge of them. Those who remain in darkness involuntarily, because they had no chance to hear about these things, may benefit from Divine Grace and not be blamed and punished for their wrong deeds.

This question brings to mind the difference between the early and present-day Muslims, and our duties toward non-Muslims. The first Muslims lived Islam fully, represented and spread it over a large area, and thereby awakened humanity's collective conscience. When we read their biographies, we see such greatness in their thinking and living that it becomes obvious why those who came into contact with them embraced Islam. They were so fearless and indomitable, so unconcerned with the pleasures and sufferings of worldly life, that they made a lasting impression upon the world.

Thanks to their sincerity and zeal, many people learned of Islam within a very short time. By the time of Caliph 'Uthman (ruled 644-56), Islam had spread from the Straits of Gibraltar to the Aral Sea, from Anatolia to the Great Wall of China. During the time of Mu'awiya (ruled 661-80), Muslims reached the Atlantic Ocean. All of Morocco, Tunisia, and Algeria were under the glorious flag of Islam.

Since these Muslims lived Islam in its entirety, most people in those lands loved and respected them. Their exemplary lives led many to Islam. Indigenous Christians and Jews often preferred Muslim rule to that of their co-religionists. Once when the Muslim rulers had to leave Damascus, the Christian community and its religious leaders prayed in their churches that the Muslims would not have to leave. When the Muslims left, the Christians promised to live under their rule and pay the due tax if they could return.[73]

The sincerity of these Muslims brought many people into Islam. Indeed, it is impossible to imagine how it could have been otherwise when those people saw the early Muslims, for each of them was an "'Umar" in sincerity and commitment. They kept long vigils during the night, and were legendary warriors on horseback during the day. They won over so many hearts and impressed people that all believed the whole world would soon belong to Islam.

Today, Muslims cannot provide security even in a small area for just their own community. Given this, the achievements of early Muslim administrations can be seen in their true light and greatness. In return for their security, reliability, wisdom, subtlety of mind and piety, the doors of many castles and cities were opened to them—not as honorary title-holders or visitors, but as governors and rulers.

When the Muslims took over Syria and Palestine, the commanders asked for the keys to Masjid al-Aqsa. The Patriarch told them that he would give them only to the person described in their holy books, for only that man was worthy to receive them. While they were disputing, Caliph 'Umar and one of his servants set out from Madina. No one knew how he would travel. But the Patriarch and priests knew how the rightful holder of keys would come.

---

[73] This incident took place when the Muslim governor abandoned the area because he believed that he could not defend it against the on-coming Byzantine army. Upon their departure, the Muslim authorities returned the taxes that had been collected for the population's communal protection. When the Muslims were able to return, the indigenous population gladly resubmitted to Muslim rule.

'Umar borrowed a camel from the state treasury, and he and his servant took turns riding it. When the Muslim commanders heard of this, they prayed that 'Umar would be riding when they had to cross the Jordan river. They thought that, as the Byzantines were used to pomp and magnificence in their rulers, 'Umar might shame himself if he were leading the camel upon which his servant was riding, and crossing the river with rolled-up trousers.

In fact, most political pomp is injustice and inequity, and 'Umar was trying to avoid it. What his commanders feared came to pass. 'Umar's garment, worn and battered by the journey, also had many patches on it. When the Patriarch saw 'Umar, he cried out: "This is the man whose description we have in our books! Now, I shall give him the key." Because of the special knowledge obtained from their books, the priests knew how 'Umar would look and how he would cross the river. Handing the key and Masjid al-Aqsa to the Muslims caused many people to embrace Islam.

With whole-hearted ardor, 'Uqba ibn Nafi' set forth to spread the word of Islam. The conquest of Africa fell to his lot. After successive victories, some people envied his fame and misinformed the Caliph about him. The Caliph was provoked, and 'Uqba was dismissed from his post, arrested, and kept from spreading Islam. Imprisoned for 5 years, his only sorrow and great longing were expressed thus: "I wish I could have spread Islam all over Africa. I was prevented from achieving this. That is the only thing I regret."

Freeing and then appointing 'Uqba governor of Africa, Yazid made it possible for him to relaunch the conquest of Africa and spread Islam. 'Uqba reached the Atlantic Ocean in a single campaign. He could not help riding his horse into the ocean and crying out: "O God! If this dark sea had not prevented me going further, I would carry Your Holy Name overseas!"

I relate these historical accounts to remind us of how Islam was represented in the past and how it is now. The early Muslims took present-day Azerbaijan, Iran, Iraq, North Africa, Bukhara, Tashkent, Samarkand—places that would produce Bukhari, Muslim, Tirmidhi, Ibn Sina, al-Farabi, Biruni [74] within 25 years. These early Muslims carried Islam to almost every part of the then-known world, and made the glorious flag of *There is no god but God, Muhammad is His Messenger* wave over many lands.

As for ourselves, we scarcely can speak the Truth to our neighbors, let alone go to foreign lands and tell the people there. Some of our neighbors may be willing to listen, but we cannot persuade even them. Our words come back to us cold, as if from walls of ice. They leave our mouths but do not penetrate the hearts and souls of people.

We point this out only to draw attention to the immeasurable distance between ourselves and the Companions. They conveyed Islam to all peoples and lived only to do this. When they could not do so, they felt sorrow and pain for the lands and people unaware of the Truth.

By contrast, we cannot represent Islam fully in our individual lives, and still less can we convey its message to people abroad. We have neither abandoned our personal needs and preoccupations, nor given the highest priority to working in the way of God. We remember the ways to our homes, our jobs, and our worldly lives only too well. Those of us who went to non-Muslim countries did so for economic reasons,

---

[74] Several of the most important figures in Islamic history.

not to take the name of God to those lands. That is why we are so unable to spread Islam among them.

If non-Muslims are now lost in deviation, corruption, and unbelief due to our own ignorance, laziness, and incompetence, we shall be called to account for it. Giving lectures and organizing seminars and panels can be considered moving toward being on the way of God, not true service to Islam. If true service to Islam is likened to a great palace, we are still wandering around the first entrance. Because we have not yet entered upon the task, many people are going astray. Sometimes we speak to them of Islam, but we have not saved ourselves from futile internal disputes and conflicts.

We are nowhere near representing Islam at the level of 'Umar, 'Uqba ibn Nafi', and others of that caliber. Who knows how their opponents were struck with awe at seeing their determined courage and indomitable devotion to God; or struck with wonder by their reliability, generosity, justice, and humanity, all of which moved them to wonder about and then embrace Islam. The fact that many of the countries in which Muslims now live were conquered by these early Muslims shows what absolute sincerity in the way of God can achieve.

Considered from this angle, the question of non-Muslims, especially those living in non-Islamic countries, takes on a different aspect. We need to see them with a greater tolerance, and say: 'Shame on us! We have not been able to convey Islam to them so that they can leave the darkness in which they live." It will help to narrate here the true story of a German family.

A Turkish worker lived with a German family. He paid great attention to his religious duties, and performed them sensitively. Except for working hours, whenever he was with the German family he told them about Islam. After a while, the father became Muslim. His wife said to him, as did the wife of 'Amir ibn Tufail: "We have always been together so far. Let's be together in the future, too, together on the Sirat Bridge and also in Paradise. If Islam really makes one reach heavenly realms, as you said, why should I stay back from such a blessing while you enjoy it?" So she embraced Islam. The children followed her, and the family group of Islam was completed and the home became an outpost of Paradise.

Several days later, the husband came and said these startling words to the Turkish worker: "I could not express my love and gratitude to you, because you have been an honored guest to us. However, sometimes I get very angry and wish to beat you up. You came and the Qur'an, the Prophet, and God followed you. My home became a heavenly abode. But I had a father. He was a very straight, good man. He passed away a few days before you came. Why couldn't you have come a bit earlier and told him of Islam as well?"

These words indeed represent the voice, the complaint, the rebuke of the whole non-Muslim world. We have failed to take Islam to them. Even in our own countries we have been unable to exert enough effort or support the cause of Islam to make our own people know it properly.

Another aspect of the question is this: Those who took us away from Islam always promised a Western standard of life. But 150 years later we are still beggars at the doors of the West. Little has changed, and we cannot say that we have progressed in any important sense. The West continues to treat us as servants who leave their countries in return for poor wages. Even if we presented its people with the golden principles of Islam, the message that will open the gates of Paradise for them, they will reject both Islam and us. In part, this is because we are despised laborers at their disposal. As usual, the rich have difficulty imagining that they need anything from the beggars at their doors.

Muslims have been defeated in so many fields many times over, and remain dependent on the West. Why should the West listen to us? Only if we can live and represent Islam thoroughly, go to the non-Muslims with a commanding confidence in our own honor, dignity, and greatness and only for the sake of God, can we hope that they will listen to us and accept Islam. We cannot continue to accept our negative image in their eyes, but how can we change this unless we regain and reassert our former identity?

In the Hereafter they will be asked why they did not embrace Islam, and we will be asked why we did not convey it to them. So, the responsibilities of both Muslims and non-Muslims should be considered equal. Any judgments about non-Muslims should be made justly and uprightly. We cannot condemn non-Muslims to Hell simply for being non-Muslims, nor can we dream that people will embrace Islam just because we ask them to do so.

We believe that the global balance will change in the near future. Especially in Turkey, Turkish Central Asia, Egypt, Pakistan, and some other places, Muslims will regain their consciousness and raise up strong individuals who will resemble the early Muslims in their desire to establish Islam and its high values in other lands. Only through sustained and sincere effort will Islam once again become a major and respected factor in the world, and will the voices of its followers be heard. This is not impossible. Those who will realize it will be Muslims of good character whose souls have bonded with Islam, not those inconsistent and inadequate Muslims who follow their bodily needs and desires and only concern themselves with Islam once in a while.

Why are there fortunate and unfortunate people?

God bestows material wealth and poverty upon individuals for reasons known only to Him. For example, a poor person might inherit wealth when a rich family member or relative dies. Some people inherit intelligence, shrewdness, and business acumen, while others who could undertake these responsibilities successfully are denied the chance to do so.

The Prophet is reported to have said that God bestows this world's goods upon whomever He pleases, but knowledge only upon those who petition Him for it. This *hadith*, although defectively transmitted, is most significant. Clearly, material possessions should not be seen as necessarily good in themselves. God does not always bestow material security and happiness upon those who ask Him for such things.

There is good in whatever He bestows. For the faithful individual who does good deeds and gives in charity some of what has been bestowed, wealth is a means of good. If, however, the individual is of weak faith and has strayed from the path of right action and charity, wealth becomes a means of evil. For someone who has deserted the path of right action, poverty might be just the excuse needed to engage in inner or outer (or both) rebellion against God. Those who do not submit totally to God, or who do not try sincerely to act upon the teachings of Islam, will find their wealth a means of distress, a severe and demanding test: *Know that your children and your worldly goods are but a trial and a temptation, and that God's reward is great* (8:28).

We should recall here a saying of the Prophet: "Among you are such people that if they raise their hands and swear by God, He grants them whatever they want and never makes them swear falsely. Bara ibn Malik is one of them." [75] This man, the younger brother of Anas, lived a life of complete poverty at the barest level of subsistence, not having enough food or a place to sleep. Although poor and ragged in appearance, such people were the most loved and appreciated for their sincere piety. They were praised, and their actions were esteemed in the Prophet's assurance that they were among those whose promises God Himself keeps.

It is recorded that once when 'Umar entered the Prophet's room, he saw upon the Prophet's back the marks of the rough matting upon which he had been sleeping. He began to cry, asking why the Byzantine and Persian emperors lived in such pomp and luxury while the Messenger slept on so rough a bed. The Prophet replied: "Don't you agree that they should have this world and we the Hereafter?" [76] Years later during his caliphate, when the treasuries of these two empires flowed into the Muslim treasury, 'Umar continued to live a life of bare subsistence.

It is not poverty in itself that is good, but rather the state of mind that has disciplined (and triumphed over) the worldly self and set its sight upon eternal life. Poverty may be a means to achieve that state of mind. But in some people it leads to inner distress, rancor, and ingratitude toward God, which is a root of unbelief. Similarly, affluence and material security may delude certain people into pride and self-esteem, causing them to neglect the needs of others and their debt to God. Such arrogance and ingratitude also is a root of unbelief.

---

[75] Bukhari, *Sulh,* 8; Muslim, *Qasama,* 24.

[76] Ibn Maja, *Zuhd,* 11.

The surest way for believers to progress is to understand that whatever God gives is designed to perfect them. Regardless of personal circumstances, believers should strive to improve the welfare of others and trust inwardly and outwardly in the All-Mighty and All-Merciful. The best attitude toward this world, which is only a resting place on the way to our everlasting destination, is expressed in this brief poem:

> I accept, my Lord, whatever comes to me from You,
> For whatever comes to me from You is my good;
> Whether a robe of honor comes or a shroud,
> Whether a sharp thorn or a sweet, fresh rose,
> If it comes with Your blessing,
> it is my good that comes.

Why are some people created "more equal" than others?

God created each one of your cells, as well as those of all other animate and inanimate parts of creation, and gave us our human nature. He has given us everything; we have given Him nothing. So how can you complain or accuse Him of being unjust? Injustice comes from not giving what is due. But we are not "due" anything, for since we have given Him nothing it is impossible for Him to owe us anything.

God, the All-Mighty, created each of us out of nothing. Moreover, He created us human, when He could have created us as something else or not at all. If you observe and investigate your surroundings, you can see many creations that are different from you. Whether they are inferior or superior to you is a matter of your own judgment.

Another aspect is the Providence of God. God may deprive individuals of something they value in order to grant them a manifold return in the Hereafter. In this way, God makes people feel their need, powerlessness, and poverty.

This causes them to turn to Him with a greater sincerity and a fuller heart, thereby becoming worthier of His Blessing and Favor. Thus your apparent loss is really a gain. This is comparable to martyrdom, which God rewards with Paradise. Martyrs attain such a rank on the Day of Judgment that even the most righteous and sincere long for it and wish that they had been martyred. What such people receive in eternity is infinitely greater and more valuable than what they lose here.

Although some disadvantaged or disabled people may blame God for their disabilities, and thereby stray from or abandon their faith, many more are strengthened in their faith. It is completely mistaken to use an exaggerated—indeed false—sympathy with the disabled as a pretext for unbelief. It is far better—even essential—that an ardent yearning for eternal life be aroused in such people, for then they can become worthy of an immense reward in the Hereafter.

If the disabilities of some lead others who enjoy good health to recognize that they have much to be thankful for and to improve themselves, their humanity, and their closeness to God, the Wisdom in Divine Providence is confirmed and, to the degree possible, understood.

Are the manner and time of death predetermined?

Every event, including the manner and time of death, are predestined. Everything occurs within the framework of the Divine Decree, and also within an individual plan for each being. Such plans are always in harmony with one another. This is a system established by God in the past eternity. It never changes, and will continue in the future eternity.

The established and universally acknowledged principles of the positive sciences confirm that everything has been made and runs according to such a design and determination. In the absence such predestination, the universe's order, harmony, and magnificence could not be understood or explained, nor could any scientific advances be made. God's preordained, mathematical, and geometrical design in the universe allows us to conduct laboratory research via reliable principles so that we can explore both humanity and space.

Saying that science is no more than a means to reflect and make known what already exists, to give some names and titles to its governing principles, does not diminish its discoveries or technological inventions. By pointing out science's place and weight, we only recall the significant fact that such order and harmony prevailed long before any scientific discoveries and inventions were made, for the Creator made them the very foundation of the universe.

Some sociologists attempt to apply to humanity principles that seem to prevail for all other beings. This is extreme fatalism, which deserves to be criticized severely. And yet it may be helpful to the extent that it acknowledges the very predestination on which the universe and its order depend.

Each fact related to faith and creed does not need human support or acceptance, or human acknowledgment of its reasonableness, because it comes from God. However, it helps our cause of calling people back to the right path if we can counter their claims. That is why we engage in such a discourse. Otherwise, it is obvious that everything functions according to a perfect balance, harmony, and order, all of which suffices to prove their predestination by an All-Mighty Sovereign. Since existence began, they have acted in full obedience and submission to His Will, Power, and Preordaining.

Predestination has a different essence for humanity. Although we were created by necessity and at the same time as other creatures, our free will makes us unique. God gave us the moral freedom to think, reason, form opinions, and make choices so that we would have personality, individuality, and character. Indeed, the question only arises because some people consider humanity to be the same as any other member of creation.

We have a real (although limited) free will, power of choice, and inclination. Depending on how we use these, we earn good or evil, reward or punishment. As we bring the results of our deeds upon ourselves through our own conscious or unconscious choices, we cannot blame God for what we ourselves set in motion. The ratio of reward or punishment to a particular deed is up to God.

There is a second aspect: How is human free will reconciled with God's all-encompassing knowledge?

In His knowledge, existence and all that is beyond it are not bound by the human concept of "time." Thus, such human concepts as "before," "after," "cause," and "effect" have no meaning and do not occur in what we consider to be the proper sequence. Simply stated, they just are. As a result, God is simultaneously aware of our inclination, what we will do, what we do, and what the result will be. This fact is a recognition of our free will, because our inclination is taken into account and given importance. In other words, God reveals that He will create whatever we incline toward and, as He foresees the consequences, predetermines those consequences accordingly. This means that He accords full importance to our free will. No one is forced to follow a prescribed course, and so everyone can be held accountable for what they do.

Fate and predetermination operate according to God's knowledge. To foreknow something does not determine or cause it to be or to happen as it does. Divine Will and Power make things come into existence on the basis of our inclination. Therefore, the things that happened and came into existence did not do so because they were foreknown. On the contrary, they are known as they are. The same is true of predestination. For example, a weather forecaster does not "cause" the weather by "predicting" it accurately. God All-Mighty's Power to foreknow and foresee the outcomes of choices and inclinations, and thus to assure that they will be fulfilled, does not mean that He causes them.

I end this discussion with one more example. Some people say that murderers cannot be held accountable for their deed, because they were "predestined" to do it and the victim was "predestined" to die in that manner. Such a claim is ludicrous. The truth is that God takes their inclinations into account, prepares the circumstances according to how they will act, and is perfectly fair in calling them to account for their heinous sin.

Why are whole nations no longer punished?

Both the Bible and the Qur'an relate how God destroyed the people of Prophet Lot and Prophet Noah. Noah's people refused to abandon their idolatry and evil ways and embrace Islam, even though he called upon them do so for centuries, and so God destroyed them by a great flood. Lot's people consistently ignored his warnings to abandon their lustful and perverted ways, and so God destroyed them with fire and brimstone.

To answer this question, we have to go back in history. Beginning with Adam, the first man, God has sent Prophets to invite His servants to the right path and eternal bliss. All Messengers were responsible only for their own people. However Prophet Muhammad, the last Prophet, was sent for all humanity and creation. His people, defined as all Muslims regardless of when and how they embraced Islam, are known as his community.

Today, many Muslims and non-Muslims are committing sins that were unheard of during earlier times. But since the Prophet was sent to humanity, we are shielded from the total annihilation or punishment visited upon earlier peoples: *But God will not send them a punishment while you are among them. Nor is He going to send it while they continue to ask for pardon* (8:33).

Another Qur'anic verse enlightens us about his mission's generality and comprehensiveness as well as the greatness and significance of his person. Jesus is quoted as entreating on behalf of his people: *If you punish them, they are Your servants—If you forgive them, You are the Exalted in Power, the Wise* (5:118). On the other hand, the All-Mighty said to Prophet Muhammad: "I will not send a punishment while you are among them and while they ask for My forgiveness."

Thus the Prophet's community has two important shields against Divine Wrath: the Prophet's physical (during his lifetime) and spiritual (after his death) presence, and the existence of sincere believers who seek His forgiveness and are allowed to do so by those in power.[77]

---

[77] Ibn Hanbal, *Musnad,* 2:159.

Many *hadith* record the Prophet's frequent pleading for his community's salvation.[78] One such prayer was made at 'Arafat and Muzdalifa during his Farewell Pilgrimage. There he asked God, among other things, not to punish his community. Some of his prayers were accepted and some were not. His Companions narrated his words as follows:

> I asked God not to send a Divine Punishment upon my community. He accepted my prayer and replied: "I will not send a punishment upon them, but they will cause destruction among themselves. If they become sinners, I will let them quarrel and fight among themselves." Then I asked God again to lift such things from my community, but He did not agree to this.

In conclusion, whole peoples will not be destroyed as long as sincere believers among the sinful multitudes worship and serve God, spread His Name and Word, seek His forgiveness, and strive to reform themselves and others.

---

[78] *Muslim*, "Hajj," 147; *Al-Bidaya wa al-Nihaya*, 5:159.

CHAPTER 7

Death

Everyone has an inborn feeling for eternity. Although confined within this transient material world, we yearn for eternity. When we listen to our inner nature, we hear it pronouncing eternity over and over again. If we were given the whole universe, it would not compensate us for our hunger for the eternal life for which we were created. Our natural inclination toward eternal happiness comes from the objective reality and existence of an eternal life and from our desire for it.

What is death?

The body is an instrument of the spirit, which governs and controls it in its entirety.

When its appointed hour comes, an illness or failure of bodily functions is like an invitation to the Angel of Death, known as Archangel 'Azra'il in Islam. God is obviously the One Who causes people to die. But to save people from complaining about Him, as death appears as a disagreeable event to many people, God uses 'Azra'il as a veil between Himself and the taking of souls. He also puts illnesses or some other calamity as another veil between 'Azra'il and death so that people are saved from complaining about him.

What about the angel of death?

Since all angels were created from light, they can be present in any place and in any form simultaneously. They also can perform countless tasks at the same time. Therefore, 'Azra'il can take millions of souls simultaneously and without any confusion. Each Archangel has subordinates that resemble him and are supervised by him. When believers die, angels come to them with smiling, radiant faces. They are followed by 'Azra'il, 'Azra'il and his subordinates charged with taking these souls, or by one of his subordinates. The Qur'anic verses: *By those who pluck out violently; by those who draw out gently* (79:1-2) indicate that the angels who take the souls of believers differ from those who take the souls of unbelievers. The souls of the latter, who have embittered and frightened faces at death, are plucked out violently.

What do we feel at the time of death?

At the time of death, believers experience the opening of windows from their places in Paradise. Prophet Muhammad stated that the souls of such people are drawn out as gently as the flowing of water from a pitcher. Better than that, martyrs do not feel death's agonies of and do not realize that they are dead. Instead, they think that they have been transferred to a better world and enjoy perfect happiness.

Prophet Muhammad told Jabir, the son of 'Abd Allah ibn 'Amr, who was martyred at the Battle of Uhud:

> Do you know how God welcomed your father? He welcomed him in such an indescribable manner that neither eyes have seen it, nor ears heard it, nor minds conceived of it. Your father said: "O God, return me to the world so that I can explain to those left behind how pleasant martyrdom is." God replied: "There is no longer a return. Life is lived only once. However, I'll inform them of your circumstances you are in," and He revealed: *Never think of those slain in the way of God as dead; rather, they are alive and are provided in the Presence of their Lord* (3:169). If you led a good, right-

eous life, you will have a happy death. If you led a
wicked life, you will have a wicked death.

Prophet Muhammad, the most advanced in worshipping
God, and 'Umar advised performing the prescribed prayers
while one is dying. Khalid ibn Walid, one of the few invinci-
ble generals in world history, asked those beside his deathbed to fetch his sword and horse. Such people as 'Uthman,
'Ali, Hamza, Mus'ab ibn 'Umayr, and many others dedicated themselves to the cause of Islam and so died as martyrs.

Should we fear death?

Those who believe and do righteous deeds have no reason to fear death. Although it appears to us as decomposition
and the extinction of life and its pleasures, in fact it is no
more than a discharge from the heavy duties of worldly life,
a change of residence, and a transferal of the body. It is an
invitation to and the beginning of everlasting life.

As the world is continually enlivened through acts of creation and predetermination, so is it continually stripped of life
through other cycles of creation, determination, and wisdom.
The death of plants, the simplest level of life, is a work of
Divine artistry, like their life—in fact, it is more perfect and
better designed. When a fruit pit dies underground, it seems
to decompose and rot away. But in fact, it undergoes a perfect
chemical process, passes through predetermined states of re-
formation, and ultimately grows again into an elaborate, new
tree. This shows clearly that death is the beginning of a new
and more elaborate life.

The "death" of fruits, vegetables, and animal flesh in a
person's stomach causes them to rise to the degree of human
life. Thus, their death can be regarded as more perfect than
their lives. Since the death of plants is so perfect and serves
such a great purpose, our own deaths must be even more per-

fect and serve a still greater purpose. After all, we occupy the highest level of life. Given this, we certainly will be brought into eternal life.

Death discharges us from the hardships of worldly life. This turbulent, suffocating, and narrow dungeon, which becomes more difficult to endure with the onset of old age and illness, admit us into the Eternal, Beloved One's infinitely wide circle of the mercy. There, we will enjoy the everlasting company of our loved ones and the consolation of a happy, eternal life.

What happens to the spirit?

Following death, each person's spirit is taken to God's Presence. If it led a good, virtuous life and became refined, the angels charged with taking it to His Presence wrap it in a piece of satin and take it, through the heavens and all inner dimensions of existence, until they reach His Presence.

Along the way, angels at all stations welcome it and ask: "Whose spirit is this? How beautiful it is!" The angels conveying it introduce it with the most beautiful titles it acquired in the world: "This is the spirit of that one who (for example) prayed, fasted, gave alms and bore all kinds of hardship for God's sake." Finally, God Almighty welcomes it and then orders the angels: "Take this back to the grave where its body is buried, so that it can answer the questions of Munkar and Nakir, the interrogating angels."

The spirit of a wicked person is treated with disdain everywhere it passes, and is thrown back to the grave after being presented to God's Presence.

Whatever evil happens in the world is due to our own sins. If sincere believers cannot always resist the temptation to sin, out of His Mercy God allows some misfortunes to strike them so that they may be purified thereby. God may also subject them to severe death agonies in order to forgive some of their sins or to promote them to higher (spiritual) ranks. In any case, their spirits are taken very gently. If there are still some sins that need to be forgiven, the believers will suffer some sort of punishment in the grave and then be freed from Hell's punishment. In addition, since the grave is the first station toward eternal life, where everyone will receive what they have earned, it is also the place of preliminary interrogation. While in their graves, everyone will be questioned by two angels about their worldly deeds. And almost everyone, except the Prophets, will undergo some suffering.

As is recorded in reliable books, 'Abbas (the Prophet's uncle) wanted to see 'Umar in a dream. However, he only saw him 6 months later. When 'Abbas asked 'Umar where he had been, the latter replied: "Don't ask! I've only just now finished accounting (for my life.)"

Sa'd ibn Mu'adh was one of the greatest Companions. When he died, Gabriel told the Messenger: "The Divine Throne trembled because of Sa'd's death." Innumerable angels took part in his funeral. After his burial, the Messenger spoke in amazement: "Glory to God! What (will happen to others) if the grave squeezes even Sa'd?"

In the grave, everyone is questioned by the angels Munkar and Nakir, who ask such questions as: Who is your Lord? Who is your Prophet? What is your religion? Believers can answer these questions with great ease; unbelievers cannot. These questions are followed by others dealing with the person's life.

The relation between the spirit and its body differs according to the worlds in which they live. In this world, the spirit is confined within the body. If the evil-commanding self and bodily desires dominate the spirit, the spirit will deteriorate and doom the person. But if the spirit can discipline the evil-commanding self through belief, worship and good conduct, and free itself from servitude to bodily desires, it is refined and acquires purity and laudable qualities. This will bring happiness to the spirit in both worlds.

After burial, the spirit waits in the intermediate world, the world between this one and the Hereafter. Although the body decomposes into the ground, its essential particles do not rot. According to a *hadith*, this is the coccyx (*ajb al-dhanab*) We do not know whether this term refers to a person's genes. But regardless of part it is, the spirit will use it to maintain its relation with the body. This part will also serve as a foundation upon which God will re-create us on the Day of Judgment. God will make the elements of this foundation conducive to eternal life while destroying and re-creating the world and resurrecting us on the Day of Resurrection.

What does the spirit do in the intermediate world? The intermediate world is the realm where the spirit feels the "breath" of the bliss of Paradise or the punishment of Hell. Those who led virtuous lives will be met by their good deeds (e.g., prayers, recitations, charity, etc.) in the form of amiable companions. Windows will be opened so that they can see heavenly scenes. And, as stated in a *hadith,* the grave will be like one of Paradise's gardens. However, even these people will suffer some punishment if they have some unforgiven sins, for such punishment will purify them of all sins and make them worthy of Paradise after the Resurrection.

Unbelievers will be met by their If unbelief and evil deeds, which will assume the forms of bad companions and such vermin as scorpions and snakes. They will be shown scenes of Hell and will experience the grave as one of Hell's pits.

Do some bodily parts or cells remain alive after death? While we live in this world, it is our spirits that suffers pain and feel joy and happiness. The spirit seems to feel pain through the nervous system, and uses this system to communicate with all bodily parts. Just how it does this remains a mystery to science, as does the type of interaction going on between the spirit and the body, especially the brain. Any bodily failure that results in death terminates the functioning of the nervous system. However, scientists have established that certain cells brain continue to live for a while after death. Scientists have studied the post-death signals received from the brain. If they can decipher such signals, such fields .as criminology will benefit greatly when it comes to solving "unsolvable" crimes.

The following verses, which tell us how God revived a dead person during the time of Moses, suggests this:

> When Moses said to his people: "God commands you to sacrifice a cow" ... they sacrificed her, a thing they had scarcely done. And when you killed a living soul, and disputed thereon, God disclosed what you were hiding so We said: "Smite him with part of it." Even so He brings to life the dead, and He shows you His signs, that haply you may have understanding. (2:67, 72-73)

Torments of the grave and Hell. Given the above understanding of the spirit, and the fact that it will remain in contact with the body's essentials particles while in the intermediate world, it is meaningless to discuss whether the spirit, the body, or both will suffer in the grave. However, as pointed out above, God will rebuild people on the Day of the Resurrection from or with those essential bodily particles, and they will be resurrected on the "morning" of the eternal life.

Since the spirit lives the worldly life together with the body and shares all its joys and griefs, God will resurrect people both bodily and spiritually. The Ahl al-Sunna wa al-Jama'a (the majority of Muslims) agree that the spirit and the body will go to either Paradise or Hell together. God will build bodies in forms peculiar to the Hereafter, where everything will be alive: *This life of the world is but a pastime and a game. Lo! the home of the Hereafter, that is life if they but knew* (29:64).

What gifts we can send to the spirit after death? The spirits in the intermediate world will see and hear us, provided God allows this. He may even permit some saintly people to see, hear, and communicate with them.

After we die, our record of deeds is not closed. If we leave behind good, virtuous children, books, or institutions from which people continue to benefit, or if we have brought up people beneficial to humanity or contributed to their upbringing, our reward will continue to increase. If, we leave behind only evil things, our sins will continue to increase as long as they harm others.

So, if we want to benefit our loved ones who have gone to the other world, we should be good heirs. We should help the poor, take part in Islamic services, and lead a good and virtuous life, and spend what they left us to promote Islam and help those who need some help, whether Muslim or non-Muslim. All of these activities will cause their reward to increase.

Why does one creature's life depend on the death of another?

Just as day replaces night, spring follows winter, and autumn takes the place of summer, death follows life. The Creator, Who governs everything, does nothing in vain. He creates the most beautiful and intricate beings out of the lowest, seemingly unpromising, materials. Since it is the very nature of His creativity to bestow freshness and novelty continually upon His creation, and since He sets on and motivates everything to mature and develop, risings and settings necessarily succeed each in this world.

Before going further into the subject, let's define death. Death is not a final exhaustion of nature, an annihilation that operates of itself, or a total extinction into a void. Rather, it is a transformation, a change of place, state, and dimension; a completion of service, a release from its burden, to attain peace and ease. For every living thing, it is a sort of retreat or transition to its own essence and truth. For this reason, death is as desirable as life. It is as pleasing as meeting friends, and a blessing as great as acquiring immortality.

Materialists who do not grasp death's meaning and truth always see it as horrifying and so compose gloomy odes to it. All such people have seen and felt the same things about death, and have made the same complaints about it.

Since death is a separation from life and the living, it affects our minds and those sentiments that make us human. It is impossible to deny such an influence, to silence the heart in the face of death. Death arouses considerable tumult in our hearts and minds, though it may be short-lived. Belief in the Resurrection causes all such sorrows to be forgotten, for it is like presenting a kingdom to a person who has lost everything, or assuring a person about to be hanged of eternal life and happiness.

According to those who understand the real meaning of death, death is no more than a release from service, a change of abode, and a journey to where most of one's friends have already gone. Those who do not understand this see only its horrifying surface meaning: death as an executioner, a gallows, a bottomless pit, a dark passage into the void.

When believers begin to experience death, the beauties and rewards of Heaven begin to appear before them. When unbelievers, who are deprived of this pleasure of faith, think of death, they begin to feel the torment and fire of Hell that they nurture within their conscience. Their suffering is not just limited to their own feelings, for in their hearts they also feel the grief and suffering of all those with whom they share interests, pleasures, and concerns. Their suffering and loss of happiness increases the burden of grief for whoever regards death as a final end.

Believers consider death a release from service and life's burdens and hardships, and know that everything continues to exist in other realms (in its identity as form and idea). Thus, they view death as an advancement, a perfection, an acquisition of a higher essence and nature. Since death carries the fruit of eternal existence and bliss, it is also a great blessing and a Divine gift.

However, every advancement and perfecting, every blessing and acquisition of it, must pass through preparatory stages: close examination, molding, and purifying. Spiritual progress and the subsequent advancement to higher levels comes only through such trials and purifications. For example, crude ores perish in the purifying furnace before they yield the pure metal. Until the ores are processed in this way, they continue to exist in soil and rock, without the metal ever being tested and then presented in its true form.

If we accept this analogy, we can understand that while death appears to be a cessation, a passing into extinction or nothingness, in reality it is a passing into a higher, more elevated mode of being. When every non-sentient particle appears to move with an eager animation toward its apparent extinction, it actually is running toward the perfection prescribed for it. When oxygen and hydrogen atoms combine, they die in their separate identities only to be reborn as water, which is essential to the vitality of all living forms. Thus we can say that death is a changing of place and form, not an end or extinction. From the tiniest particles to the greatest compounds within the universe, all changes, transformations and decompositions result in what is most beautiful, fresh, and excellent. That is why we define death as the movement of beings to a higher mode rather than as their extinction.

In another respect, death is the time when one being resigns and hands over its affairs to its successor(s). This is enacted in the sight of Him Who has sovereignty and dominion over all things. Each creature is charged with presenting itself in a unique parade before the presence of the One Who gave it existence. Just before its parade is over, and the picture or record of it made and stored, the parade of its successor(s) begins, which relieves the parade ground of sameness and refreshes the scene with new and active beings. Each being acts out its role and moves aside so that others may appear, act out their roles, and show their skills. The freshness, liveliness, beauty, and excellent diversity seen in creation is the result of these comings and goings.

Death also may be understood as silent advice, in the sense that nothing is self-existent. In other words, nothing can survive by itself or has permanence. A fading and ultimately dead light indicates a source of light that is unfailing and eternal. For those who grieve and complain about the transience and perishing of all things, this is a good lesson on how to mature and attain true happiness. Whatever or whoever captivates our hearts will leave us one day, which causes us to yearn for an eternal being to love and to be loved by. In our transient world, such a yearning is the first stage of moving toward or attaining eternity. Death is the mysterious uplifter that raises people to that dignity.

Given this, we can liken death to a healing hand, one that nurses to full health, that hurts us only as a doctor would hurt us: by giving a necessary inoculation or lancing, rather than a grim sword or sickle laying everything to waste. Considering death as a merely utilitarian way of making room for new generations is mistaken, for death is not absolute annihilation or extinction. Rather, what disappears does so only from within the horizons of our limited understanding, for the identity of every particular (as form and idea) continues to exist in our memories, in the Preserved Record, and in God's all-encompassing knowledge. They also exist in different dimensions and in realms beyond those dimensions, beyond corporeal understanding. For example, seeds and flowers bloom and die, but their identity as form and idea continues in the many seeds and flowers that will bloom after them.

Consider the subject from another angle. If there were no death, would we not live in a hell of unrelieved terror as we faced an endless existence without a break or relief? How could we measure the worth or value of anyone or anything, conserve or concentrate our energy, make or carry out an intention, if time was limitless? If such a situation existed, those who now mourn the fact of transience and death would mourn their absence. Moreover, we would not experience creation's inexhaustible variety, with all the prompts and images it gives to the human mind of beauty, freshness, and loss with renewability. How, in the absence of such a panorama of novelty within stability, could the human mind be inspired to contemplate that which lies beyond and sustains the visible world? How could we seek and worship the One who creates and provides for the whole.

Let's deal with the subject from a different angle. If everything depended on life instead of death, if beings continued to live through calamities, and if all events and life followed one direction forever, what could have happened? What could happen mean?

Basing ourselves on what we said earlier, death contains blessing and wisdom. Life without death would be such an absurdity and horrible disaster that, if such a situation could be fully described, people would cry and mourn about staying alive instead of dying.

If nothing died, neither a fly nor a human being could have lived in the early ages of this world, for ants and varieties of ivy would have invaded and occupied the entire planet. Nothing else could have survived or thrived. And later on, if no ant or ivy ever died, there would have been thick layers of them covering the Earth. As such statements cannot be disputed, we can see what a great blessing death is, and the great wisdom in allowing dead things to decompose.

How much of the Earth's enthralling beauty and splendor could be seen with such a huge number of ivy plants and ants? What would this world, created to exhibit the splendor and magnificence of His art, be if such a situation prevailed? How could we witness the power, might, knowledge, and grace of the Creator and Owner of this world?

The absence of death also would give rise to another problem: The magnificent wisdom and order in the rule of this universe shows that nothing in it was created in vain. The Absolute Owner of the physical and spiritual domains creates the most worthwhile things out of what may appear to us the most worthless, making the valueless into the priceless. New and excellent creations is engendered from the cells serving as bodily forms for His servants, especially those making up the human souls that God has recalled and holds in His realms. If the bodies, which He valued so highly that He "breathed" human souls in them, were allowed to decompose into nothing, the Creator's Omniscient Wisdom would be contradicted. Any such notion is absolutely contrary to His Divine Honor, and so cannot be entertained.

In conclusion, all of creation, its balance and order, the control and administration by which its complex harmonies are sustained, is so magnificent that it inspires all people whose hearts and minds are open to the beauty and pleasure around them. The dividing, combining, and moving of atoms; the growth of plants and trees; the gushing of rivers to the sea; the oceans' expanse, grandeur, and incalculable power; the evaporation of salt water and its return as life-giving rain—everything races ardently from one stage to another, higher and better.

What a universe this is! See how restless it makes our minds! The miracles of the All-Mighty parade before my eyes. What Truth spreads out from the heavens is the heavens' smiling:

> Veils of His light in glorious
> varieties of color and shade
> In the grass, the sea, the mountains,
> the spring morning!
> Born in such a world, longing
> to be a poet is only natural.

CHAPTER 8

Various Issues

Can our intention save us?

An intention that leads to the appropriate intended action being taken may save a person. An intention that does not result in any determination to bring about the intended result cannot save a person. To have an intention means to have an aim and a purpose. It is also a state of mind and a commitment. To have a clear intention means realizing clearly what one desires and which path to follow, attaining the appropriate state of mind, and then seeking the means to achieve the envisaged purpose.

Intention is the spring of all action. Whether conscious or not, intention gives a person the right to claim responsibility for particular actions. It is also the firm ground of will and power to bring about particular results. Everything related to humanity and to the world, both in its inception and continuance, depends upon someone's intention.

Everything first comes into the mind as an idea and, depending upon whether or not one plans to bring it into reality, may later become a reality via perseverance. If Without the initial idea is not transformed into an intention, a project cannot bear any useful fruit. Without perseverance, defined as intent sustained through determination and resolve, no project can succeed.

Intention has a decisive role with regard to good and bad deeds. Its quality can act like a cure for any disease or disadvantage, or be the hidden catastrophe that destroys all accomplishments in a single moment. Deeds that appear very small and insignificant can engender huge positive or negative consequences, based solely on the underlying intention.

All actions undertaken in the consciousness of serving God, such as praying or temporarily refraining from some permitted pleasures, increase our rewards and raise us to a higher spiritual level. Of course, the reverse is also true. We please God by performing or renouncing certain actions according to His law, and thereby attain the best stature.

And yet at other times we may do exactly the same thing and have it mean nothing to God, for we do it without the proper intention. For example, martyrdom on the battlefield is one of the highest achievements in Islam. Those who hope for it but fight only out of their own whim and desire are not considered martyrs, and so do not receive that reward. On the other hand, those who consistently and sincerely ask for martyrdom but die in their own beds are considered martyrs, for they sincerely intended to defend Islam and provide a better future for Muslims. They have the right to hope for the reward of martyrdom and Paradise.

Intention is a key that opens the door of the infinite. When used properly, it opens the door to eternal happiness, for all duties performed properly and sincerely are rewarded not according to the amount of time spent on them, but according to the degree they involve and affect one's life. If this key is not used properly, it leads to eternal misery and wretchedness.

Any soldier ready for jihad, though not actually engaged in battle, is right to hope for the same reward as those actually fighting. A sentry waiting to stand guard is just as eligible for reward as the one actually standing guard. The reward for being on guard in the way of God is as much as the reward of one who prays for months.

Thus a believer may attain Paradise after a short life, while an unbeliever who has lived just as long will attain eternal punishment and misery. Otherwise, according to external justice, people must be rewarded according to the amount of their good and bad deeds, as well as their virtues or vices. This would mean that they would stay in Paradise as long as they had lived righteously, and in Hell as long as they lived evilly. But as eternity is the ultimate end for both good and bad people, eternal happiness or punishment lies in one's intention. An intention to live faithfully and righteously forever will result in eternal happiness, just as an intention to live in denial, rejection, and corruption forever will result in eternal misfortune.

If, in their last minutes of life, conscious and devoted servants of God were given the chance to live another 1,000 years, they would lead lives of the same caliber. Based on this sincere intention, it would be accepted and rewarded accordingly, for believers' intentions are more benevolent than their deeds.[80] The same would be true of unbelievers, who would continue to live their evil lives if given the same choice. So, people are rewarded or punished according to their intention. The intention to acquire true faith and to preserve it results in eternal bliss; the opposite results in eternal torment.

Satan will pay most dearly for the everlasting unbelief he encourages or nurtures. Satan has undeniable effects on people, some of which are good. As a result of his activities,

---

[80] *Majma' al-Zawa'id,* 1:69 and 1:109.

some people improve their innate capacities, discover and refine their hidden values and virtues, and become more alert and conscious.

Satan attacks individuals and peoples. By sowing poisonous seeds in our hearts, he seeks to trap us in vice and evil. Our spiritual faculties warn us against his temptations and corruption, and call us to battle, just as particular bodily cells raise the alarm and resist infection.

Just as resistance to disease improves the body's immunity, our spiritual state is strengthened by seeking refuge in the All-Mighty. Given this, we stand to gain much more benefit than harm from Satan's attacks. Any testing of the spirit increases its alertness, consciousness, and power to resist. All of these make the spirit even more determined to do what is right, and more prudent when it encounters danger. Such testing transforms warriors into veterans in the way of God, martyrs and saints, and distinguishes believers from unbelievers.

Yet Satan has no share in the reward of those who attain high virtue by struggling against him, for he intends to lead people astray and corrupt them out of spite and rancor. He is punished eternally for his evil intention and bad deeds:

> God asked: "What prevented you from bowing down when I commanded you?" Satan replied: "I am better than he. You created me from fire, and him from clay." God said: Get out. It is not for you to be arrogant here. Get out, for you are of the meanest." He said: "Give me respite till the day they are raised up." God replied: "Be among those who have respite." Satan said: "Because you have thrown me out of the Path, I will lie in wait for them on Your Straight Path." (7:12-16)

After his jealous and arrogant disobedience, Satan willfully chose the way of rebellion and unbelief. His oath to lead people astray is the beginning of our never-ending tragedy.

In sum, intention is almost everything for believers, for it can elevate our most routine acts and produce much fruit. Its quality and content opens the door to the eternal and blissful life, as well as the door to eternal punishment and misery. As we say: "Actions are judged only by intentions, and a person will have only what was intended." [81]

What is the Sunna's role today?

A *hadith* says: "There is a reward as much as that of 100 martyrdoms for one who adheres to my Sunna when my community is spoiled."

Technically, Sunna refers to the way the Prophet lived. In particular, it refers to the ways and practices he wished Muslims to follow, and to all actions and norms that he lived and recommended but did not make obligatory upon us.

This subject has been dealt with thoroughly by Islamic scholars, all of whom agree that the Sunna is the way of religion, and that it is like a staircase or a ladder to reach the Truth, one of God's Names. It is a way of such merit that all systems and their principles, even those established by scholars and saints, are seen as slight, dim, and obscure beside it. All mystics, spiritual teachers, and truth-seekers have acknowledged and spoken of the Sunna in this way, and thus encouraged everyone to follow it.

God raised the Prophets and through them revealed the proper way of life. He sent Muhammad as His last Prophet; guided him in all his acts; and conveyed *fard, wajib, sunna,* and *mustahab* acts,[82] and even manners. So, one who strives

---

[81] Bukhari, *Bad'u al-Wahy,* 1; Muslim, *Imara,* 155; Abu Dawud, *Talaq,* 11.

[82] Various classes of mandatory or recommended actions.

to live as the Prophet did draws closer to God and attains a degree as described in this *hadith al-qudsi*:

> My servants do not draw near to Me with anything more loved by Me than the religious duties I have imposed upon them. They continue to draw near to Me with supererogatory works so that I shall love them. When I love them, I am their hearing with which they hear, their seeing with which they see, their hands with which they grasp, and their feet with which they walk.[83]

One meaning of this is that God enables such believers to see the true reality of things, and so makes it possible for them to evaluate things correctly and efficiently. By opening new gates and new horizons, God leads them to the truth.

Such believers easily take wing and fly toward guidance as they escape from error and corruption. When they hear a voice calling to the truth, they come to themselves, regain enthusiasm, acquire lofty aspirations, make resolutions, and start to prosper morally and spiritually. When they speak, God makes them speak the truth. When they do something, God directs them to good and beneficial results, and never leaves them alone with their self. Since these servants seek His approval and pleasure, God grants them the opportunities and enables them to act according to His Divine Pleasure.

Therefore, God controlled and guided the lives of all Prophets, blocked all ways except the one leading to His Pleasure, prevented them from choosing ways other than His Own, and directed them to the sole Sunna. So many people have followed the Sunna that it has become the clear road to salvation, the only way free of deviation and leading to success and happiness in this world and the next.

---

[83] Bukhari.

At a time when malice, depravity, and intrigue are so widespread, trying to revive and restore the Sunna, to practice it alongside *fard* and *wajib*, to assure its central place in any future society, and to make it endure until the Day of Judgment are actions of the highest importance. Such actions raise those who sincerely work for them to the rank of martyrs and assure them of an equal reward. To gain the rewards of two martyrs would be blessing enough, but more is promised. Further, those who strive to revive the truths of faith may earn rewards far greater than those of 100 martyrs.

Reviving certain elements of the Sunna is particularly worthy of the high rewards promised. For instance, one kind of slanderous gossip is worse than adultery or murder.[84] There is an obvious difference between slandering an individual and a whole community. In such a case, a personal sin can lead to widespread evil. At a time when Muslims are being invited to depravity, and when Islam's power, influence, and spread are being prevented and undermined, those who strive to restore any aspect of the Sunna will earn the reward of many martyrdoms. If their sincere efforts coincide with the holy days, nights, and months in Islam, their reward may be still greater, for God bestows much more favor upon whom He wills.

Those who serve God are favored and blessed. In their struggle to revive Islamic thought and life at a time when everything is done to oppose Islam, to work for establishing sound institutions with sincere and able staffs, to raise young people's Islamic consciousness—these are parts of a unique task that can be considered a continuance of the Prophet's mission. If such great people and spiritual guides as 'Abd al-

---

[84] Daylami, 3:116.

Qadir al-Jilani and others appeared, after so many ages, to give moral support, it is because of the great significance and need of the duties to be undertaken.

The Prophet has been seen in dreams watching over, supporting, and giving glad tidings to those on his way. Although no less than a miracle of the Sunna in the service of Sunna, we must not consider such things as recognition of someone's merits and virtues.

Certain individuals, groups, and institutions engaged in this effort surely will obtain a great share of His grace and blessing. This must be so, for "one who caused [an event] is like the doer," and it is another aspect of the vastness of Divine Favor. On the other hand, the responsibility and the trust will be removed from such workers who do not maintain their initial purity, sincerity, enthusiasm, and momentum. Some may be refused, excluded, and even forsaken by Providence, and the trust will be passed to those who are more deserving.

Only if we realize and appreciate God's favor, try to do sincerely whatever we can, and make the best use of the opportunities open to us can we prove ourselves worthy of more and greater favors from God.

Why is atheism so widespread?

Atheism means denying God's existence, which of course involves rejecting His commandments, as well as religious reflection and seriousness, and believing in the possibility of total self-independence apart from God. As such beliefs negate the concept of sin, people imagine that they can live as they please. Therein lies in the corruption of people's hearts and minds. Atheism spreads because education is misused, young people are neglected, and schools actually defend and foster it.

Ignorance about the essentials of faith and religion is the primary reason why atheism starts to grow and develop. People whose minds, hearts, and souls have not been directed to the truth inevitably become vulnerable. Only God's help and grace can save them. If a community does not confront this trend decisively and successfully, its members' hearts and minds become open to other influences that lead to deviation.

Atheism first manifests itself as a lack of interest in the principles of faith. People with this attitude often claim that it is positive, for it represents a desire for the mind's independence and freedom of thought. As the demands of faith are strenuous, indifference turns toward what is easier. It seeks any pretext to excuse it from honest and serious reflection, and so falls easily into neglect, then heedlessness, atheism, and even contempt for religion.

In fact, atheism is neither grounded on sound reasoning nor supported by human intuition or experience. Still less is it based upon "scientific" truth. It is no more than a mood, typically lazy but sometimes active and militant, of not caring and of rebellion.

The countless manifestations of God within and outside ourselves testify that there is only One Creator and Governor who administers, directs, and sustains this universe. We may think of each manifestation as a letter or book from God to us, reflecting His Divine Attributes in a way that we can understand. These Attributes can be traced everywhere in creation, which is no more than a vast area for testing and teaching humanity. However, some people with incorrect concepts have erred greatly in their understanding and observation of these signs. As a result, they have presented nature, as well as it principles and relationships, it such a

way that many people (especially the young) have abandoned true faith.

Much has been said and written about the natural world's
delicate balance and innumerable subtle harmonies. Such an
order can be attributed only to the All-Mighty. Planets and
stars move within an interrelated complexity of drifts and
orbits that are infinitely more precise than anything we could
ever design or make. If what we make is accepted as evidence
of intelligent design, why is the far more vast and complicat-
ed universe considered an exception to this rule?

Nature resembles a huge factory of enormous (actual and
potential) generative power. Its working principles are aston-
ishingly subtle and supple, yet firmly established in reassur-
ing patterns and rhythms. From where does nature get these
operating rules? Some say that nature is self-created, but how
can that persuade anybody? Of course one of the operating
rules is a measure of self-organizing power. But we want to
know the origin of this rule.

Principles are non-essential attributes of a thing or being
and, as such, are secondary and dependent on substance and
essence. Attributes cannot exist before or independently of
the compound or organism of which they are attributes. Thus,
if a plant demonstrates a measure of self-organizing power by
seeking light, moisture, and nutrients for its growth, it means
that a measure of self-organizing power has been embedded
in its seed. Similarly, the principle of attraction in physics
operates in and through existent masses, distances, and
forces. To claim that such principles are the origin or source
of existent things or beings is untenable.

Just as untenable is the confidence with which such
claims are asserted. To claim that this extraordinarily subtle
and ordered universe is the outcome of haphazard coinci-

dences is absurd, contradictory, and quite unscientific, for all the evidence points to the exact opposite.

As the result of long experiments and reflection, Muller declared that reason could not explain the origin of life. He established, on behalf of science and scientists, the absurdity of "coincidence" as a possible explanation. Similarly, after a 22-year series of studies, the Soviet Institute of Chemistry, under the chairmanship of Oparin, proved that the laws of chemistry and chemical reactions shed no light on the origin of life, and that science still has no answer to this question.

When these scientists acknowledged the limitations to human inquiry, they did so on behalf of all science and scientists. Yet such work has not undone the damage done by earlier, less careful scientists, who offered only guesses as reliable scientific theory. Unfortunately, general attitudes and values continue to be shaped by such guesses and not by the realities established by better scientists.

For example, many textbooks and encyclopedias continue to present humanity's evolution from apes to human beings as fact instead of theory. In reality, a growing number of scientists, most particularly evolutionists, argue that Darwin's theory of evolution is not a truly scientific theory at all. Many critics of the highest intellectual caliber admit that we still have no idea of how this "evolution" took place. While there is a great deal of divergent opinion among the experts about probable causes and the actual process, the general public and less-informed scientists continue to believe in it.

Various research projects and published studies cast doubt on evolution and seek to give a truer picture of nature as creation and our place in it. Works like *Why Do We Believe in God?* help those who considered non-believers in evolution as rather odd people reconsider their opinion and reflect more wisely on the matter.

Given the fact that a sound, reliable understanding of the natural world leads to belief in a single, universal Creator, atheism has more to do with obstinacy, prejudice, and a refusal to give up illusions than with the mind's independence or freedom of thought. Young people remain vulnerable, for their understanding of their behavior's nature and consequences is incomplete, their awareness of their spiritual being and their resulting deep-seated spiritual needs is limited, and their grasp of the balance between material and non-material values that characterizes a total human existence is deficient. Thus they are easily deceived by outdated concepts presented as "scientific" truths, although scientists know (and have said) that they are no more than theories. This is why teaching and learning about the truth are more important today than other duties and obligations.

If this vital task is not taken up, we may be unable to rectify the worsening situation in the future. Some of those evil consequences are with us already. This may be the major reason for our suffering over the years. We are the unlucky generation that was deprived of good teachers—teachers who had attained inward unity and harmony of mind and heart, truly knew themselves in their deepest thoughts and feelings, desired to teach others, and were willing to suffer to promote others' happiness and welfare. We hope such noble-minded teachers will arise among us and undertake this truly humane mission to rescue people from them current moral and spiritual suffering.

If this can be done, present and future generations will acquire the necessary stability in their thinking and reasoning about life's great questions. They will be able to resist the lure of false beliefs and illusions, and thereby be saved from the anxiety of constantly doubting the nature and purpose of their lives. They will be immunized, at least partially, against atheism and its attendant self-centered and neurotic behaviors. Atheism is caused by a lack of knowledge and learning, an inability to synthesize one's inner and outer life, and is the result of an undernourished heart and soul. People cling to what they know, and resist what they do not know—or at least try to remain uninterested and unconcerned.

The mass media continually presents ideas, lifestyles, and character types that encourage self-indulgence and self-abandonment. Thus it is no surprise that many young people try to become hippies or punks or whatever the latest craze is; seek immediate gratification and pleasure; and do not bother to cultivate their minds or their tastes, but prefer triviality and banality, loudness and vulgarity.

People quickly adopt ways considered exciting and attractive. What they do not know becomes even more strange and alien, and eventually a matter of total indifference. Thus we have to find effective ways to introduce young people to the deeper ways of religious life, ways that lead away from anxiety and toward tranquillity, away from darkness and toward light.

Young people are excitable and susceptible. They crave limitless freedom and have an abundance of unsatisfied appetites and desires. Their overly generous hearts and minds cause imbalance and disharmony, which can lead them toward atheism. They prefer immediate pleasure, however slight or brief, to the misery and distress that come in the wake of indulgence. They jump at the pleasures and enjoyments that Satan displays to them, and so prepare their own calamity. They fly to the fire of atheism just as moths are drawn to light.

While ignorance and unfed hearts and souls increase, materialism and carnality gradually subvert the desire for truth and annul any nobility of purpose. This is what happened with Faust.[85] This man, who desired extraordinary powers to do whatever he wished for a limited period, sold his soul for a very cheap price to Mephistopheles, Satan's agent. But when he received these powers, his noble aims of serving humanity left him and he wasted his years of power by pursuing trivial pleasures.

When the soul is dead, the heart dies, compassion disappears, and the mind and reason become so bewildered and confused that people become helpless victims of their own passing whims or the worst fads. Anyone who becomes obsessed with carnal passion and sensuality will suffer crises and change direction continually, applaud every new fashion in thought as if it were the truth, and swing from one ideology to another—from confusion to doubt and back again. They will find no attraction in faith, in a steady sense of duty, or in a patient, enduring heart.

Nor will they find any merit in moral education, self-discipline, contemplation, the soul's improvement, or in strengthening their morals and manners. Wholly addicted to triviality and self-indulgence, they will deny any achievement to our ancestors and remain willfully ignorant of what real culture and civilization can make possible: a balance between spirituality and sanity, between virtue and happiness.

---

[85] Written by Goethe (d. 1832), this classic work is the story of a person's spiritual journey and self-discovery.

Not everyone can be saved. Therefore, we should direct our efforts toward educating those young people in whom the worst habits have not become firmly established. They must be taught the fundamental principles of the system on which we depend and to which our existence belongs. They must be led to a systematic, straight, and honest way of thinking. Those who fail in this effort will see their community or nation continue to sink into moral and spiritual corruption until it can no longer be rescued.

An additional cause of atheism is the deliberate rejection of all constraints and prohibitions. Such undesirable and unrestrained indulgence has entered Muslim societies from western Europe via a degenerate form of existentialism (mainly French) that rejected traditional values and formal religious education in favor of absolute individual freedom. The theory was that the individual would (and could) mature and develop into a noble, moral being through personal experience.

This theory, regardless of where it has been applied, has never produced sane, caring, and compassionate human beings. Rather, it has intensified misery and selfishness by isolating individuals from their families, traditions, and even from themselves. Its adherents do not cultivate their morals or tastes, but rather live shallow, private lives and make no effort to find the truth. In short, they simply survive from moment to moment in the illusory hope that they may yet find happiness.

These few reflections do not cover the whole subject. Yet I hope that future guides, teachers, and leaders with discernment and foresight will consider them when trying to stop the spread of deviation and atheism. I have presented a brief insight into the problem, with the prayer that some people may be alerted to the truth, conquer the self, and regain the means to do what is good.

What is jihad?

Jihad is an Arabic word meaning to strive, to make an effort, to face hardships of all kinds. After Islam, it came to mean striving in the way of God.

The Qur'an almost equates jihad, an important Islamic duty, with Islam. The most distinguished servants of God, whether Prophets or saints, have attained their distinction through jihad against unbelievers and against their own carnal selves. Jihad has a great worth in the sight of God, because He created us to strive so that we might discover our true being and encourage others to do likewise.

God decrees in the Qur'an:

> Those believers who sit at home, other than those who
> have a disabling hurt, are not equal with those who
> strive in the way of God with their possessions and
> their selves. God has conferred on those who strive
> with their possessions and their selves a rank over
> those who sit at home; yet to each, God has promised
> good, but He has bestowed on those who strive a great
> reward above those who sit at home. (4:95)

People have diverse careers, and their objectives in those careers allow others to assess their standing. But what is our end? Whatever our rank or occupation, each person was created from a drop of fluid and will end as a corpse.

This is true of everything but the work of Prophethood. Its reward multiplies until the Day of Judgment, for it contains some spiritual quality that is not touched by mortality. A Prophet seeks to enable people to know God and thereby reach eternity. We were not created to be subjected to physical corruption and dissolution. Our deepest natural tendency is toward eternity, and the Prophets who alert, educate, and cause us to realize this tendency.

In the sight of God, Prophethood is the most sacred work entrusted to humanity, and jihad expresses this aspect of it. Due to its importance, the Qur'an distinguishes those Muslims who swore to the Prophet that they would perform jihad:

> Those who swear allegiance to you, swear allegiance only to God. The hand of God is above their hands. So whoever breaks his oath, breaks it only at his own peril; while whoever keeps his covenant with God, on him will He bestow immense reward (48:10).

This verse was revealed when the Messenger told the Muslims they would return to Makka and make pilgrimage. So they set out as pilgrims for Makka. But when they reached Hudaibiyya, the Makkan polytheists refused to let them pass and threatened war. This unexpected objection shocked the believers, who regarded it as a heavy blow to Islam's honor. They did not know how to respond. The Messenger sent 'Uthman ibn Affan to Makka to reaffirm that they had come only to make pilgrimage and therefore in peace.[86] The Makkan chiefs imprisoned 'Uthman and circulated the rumor of his death. This news so angered the Muslims that the Prophet demanded that they swear allegiance to him by taking his hand. God then revealed the verse quoted above.

Another verse reads:

> God has bought from the believers their lives and their wealth because Paradise will be theirs. They fight in

---

[86] 'Uthman ibn 'Affan, an early convert to Islam, came from the wealthy and powerful Umayyad clan. He was chosen for this mission because he had powerful family members and relatives in Makka who could protect him. In later years, he was the third caliph of Islam, ruling from 644 to 656.

> the way of God, slay and are slain. It is a promise
> which is binding on Him in the Torah and the Gospel
> and the Qur'an. And who is more true to his promise
> than God? Rejoice then in your bargain that you have
> made, for that is the supreme triumph. (9:111)

This "bargain" is the highest distinction, since whoever enters into it is being directly addressed by God.

The Messenger said: "I wished very much that I had been slain for the cause of God and brought to life to be slain again, and brought to life to be slain again."[87] He also said: "It is better to keep one's eyes open for a day's duty, solely in the cause of God, against the danger of enemy infiltration through a pass, than to possess the world and all its contents."[88] We may infer from this hadith that to be alert for a day in the cause of God, against any danger that may befall the community, is better than possessing the Ka'ba—since the Ka'ba is among the contents of this world.

Another *hadith* tells us: "The recompense from God for one's good acts is cut off at the moment of death, except for jihad. The reward for jihad multiplies until the Day of Judgment. Further, God exempts those who have striven in His way from being interrogated in the grave."[89]

Jihad has two aspects: fighting to overcome carnal desires and evil inclinations (the greater jihad) and encouraging others to achieve the same objective (the lesser jihad). The Muslim army was returning to Madina after defeated the enemy, when the Messenger told them: "We are returning

---

[87] Bukhari, *Iman,* 26; *Jihad,* 7; Ibn Maja, *Jihad,* 3:18.

[88] Tirmidhi, *Fada'il al-Jihad,* 12.

[89] Muslim, *Imara,* 163; Ibn Maja, *Jihad,* 7.

from the lesser jihad to the greater one." When the Companions asked what the greater jihad was, he explained that it was fighting with the carnal self.[90]

The aim of either jihad is to purify believers of sin so that they may attain true humanity. The Prophets were sent for this purpose:

> Thus We have sent unto you a Messenger from among you, who recites unto you Our revelations (and makes Our signs known to you), and who purifies you of sin and teaches you the Scripture and Wisdom, and teaches you that which you did not know. (2:151)

We are like raw minerals to be worked upon by the Prophets, who purify and refine us by removing the seal from our hearts and ears, and lifting the veils from our eyes. Enlightened by the message they bring, we can understand the meaning of the laws of nature, which are signs of God's Existence and Unity, and penetrate into the subtle reality of things and events. Only the Prophets can guide humanity to the high status expected of them by God.

In addition to teaching the signs, the Prophets also instruct us in the Book and in Wisdom. As the Qur'an was the last Revelation to the Last Prophet, God means the Qur'an when He speaks of the Scripture, and the Sunna when He speaks of Wisdom. Therefore we must follow the Qur'an and the Prophet's Sunna if we desire to be rightly guided.

The Prophet also teaches us what we do not know, such as how to purify ourselves of sin, and we will continue to learn from him until the Day of Judgment. By following his way, many great Muslims became saints. One of them, 'Ali, said that his belief in the pillars of Islam was so firm that his

---

[90] *Kashf al-Khafa'*, 1:424.

certainty would not increase even if the veil of the Unseen were lifted.[91] 'Abd al-Qadir al-Jilani is said to have had insight into the mysteries of the seventh heaven. These and many others, such as Fudail ibn Iyaz, Ibrahim ibn Adham, and Bishr al-Khafi, might well have been endowed with Prophethood if God had not sent the last Prophet already.

The dark clouds of ignorance have been removed from our intellectual horizon through the Prophet's guidance, and many more scientific and technological advances will be made because of the light he brought from God.

Jihad is the legacy of the Prophets, and Prophethood is the mission of elevating people to God's favor by purifying them. This Prophetic mission is known as jihad, for it has the same meaning as bearing witness to the truth. Those who perform jihad bear witness to God's Existence and Unity by striving in His way: *God bears witness that there is no god but He and so do the angels and the people of learning, maintaining justice: there is no god save He, the All-Mighty, the Wise* (3:18). Such people also bear witness to the same truth in the heavenly court, where the case of unbelievers will be settled.

God bears witness to His own Existence and Unity, and those who have acquired a high level of perception can grasp the reality of this testimony. Angels bear witness to this, as they are absolutely pure in nature, as do those endowed with knowledge. Even if everybody were to deny God's Existence and Unity, the testimony of these groups is enough to establish this truth.

Those who bear witness to this truth should travel throughout the world to spread it. This was the duty of the Prophets, and it should be our duty as well:

---

[91] Imam Rabbani, *Maktubat,* 1:157.

Messengers who brought good news to humanity and
who admonished them, so that they might have no
argument against God after their coming. God is the
All-Mighty and the All-Wise. God Himself bears witness by what He has revealed to you that it has been
revealed with His knowledge; and so do the angels.
There is no better witness than God. (4:165-66)

God chose a man from each nation and appointed him a
Prophet. From the time of Prophet Adam, each dark era of
human history was enlightened by a Prophet's message. This
continued until the time of Muhammad, who was sent to
enlighten all people's intellectual and spiritual horizons: *We
have sent you (Muhammad) as a witness and a bearer of
good tidings and a warner* (48:8).

Prophet Muhammad is mentioned in the Qur'an as "the
Prophet". The use of the definite article distinguishes him
from all other Prophets and indicates that he is the Prophet
par excellence. He has been sent as a blessing all creation,
including animals, plants, and inanimate things.

God directly addresses Muhammad in many Qur'anic
verses and says: *We have sent you...* This means that he is the
Prophet sent by God to bear witness to His Existence and
Unity. He carried out this task during a time of ignorance,
when almost everyone denied this truth. Gradually, his followers increased until they became the global flagbearers of
this truth. Prophet Muhammad conveyed the good news of
happiness in this world and the next for those who do good,
and warnings for those who do evil. In so doing, he performed jihad.

God has sent a Prophet to each people, which means that
everyone has some idea of Prophethood. As the term used to
describe the activity of Prophethood, jihad is so deeply
engraved on the heart of every believer that they all feel a

profound responsibility to spread the truth and thereby guide others to the Straight Path.

The lesser jihad, usually understood as fighting for God's cause, does not refer only to actual fighting on the battlefield. Rather it is comprehensive, for it includes every action from speaking out to actual fighting, provided that the action is done for the sake of God. Every individual or communal action, no matter how great or small, taken to benefit humanity is included in the meaning of the lesser jihad.

While the lesser jihad depends on mobilizing all material facilities and is performed in the outer world, the greater jihad is our personal fight against our carnal selves. These two forms of jihad cannot be separated from each other, for only those who conquer their carnal selves can perform the lesser jihad, which, in turn helps us succeed in the greater jihad.

The Messenger taught us how to perform both types of jihad, and established the principles of preaching the truth that we are to follow until the Day of Judgment. His method of acting was very systematic. This is actually another proof of his Prophethood, and a wonderful example of following the way of God in behavior.

The Messenger used to pray at the Ka'ba during the first years of his Prophethood. In addition to hoping for increased rewards from God for doing so, his foremost intention was to preach the truth to young people. But it was impossible to approach them because of their haughtiness. Knowing that actions speak louder than words, he started praying at the Ka'ba. With their curiosity aroused, they asked him what he was doing and so gave him a good opportunity to preach to them.

The Prophet was attacked several times while praying. Once, Abu Jahl planned to kill him with a big stone during his prostration. Abu Jahl held the stone aloft, ready to bring it down on the Prophet, but then began to tremble, grew pale with fear, and held his hands motionless above his head. When asked what had happened, he answered that an awful monster had come between him and the Prophet, and that it almost swallowed him.[92]

On another occasion when the Prophet was praying, 'Uqba ibn Abi Mu'ait wound his turban round the Prophet's neck in an attempt to strangle him. On hearing of this, Abu Bakr hurried to the scene to save the Prophet and shouted: "Would you kill a man merely because he says: 'My Lord is God'?" [93] This was an echo of the words spoken in the time of Moses by a believer who had hurried to save him from those who wished to kill him.

The Prophet might have been martyred in any of those assaults if God had not protected him. He publicly demonstrated the importance of preaching the truth even at the risk of one's life. Abu Bakr used to recite the Qur'an loudly by the window of his house. Those who heard him would gather around him. His recitation attracted so many people that the Makkan chiefs told him to stop. Ibn Daghinnah, who had extended his protection to Abu Bakr, had to revoke it. However, Abu Bakr was determined to continue his recitation.[94]

Whether by words or actions, the Companions never stopped performing jihad, because they believed firmly that

---

[92] Muslim, *Munafiq*, 38.

[93] Bukhari, *Tafsir:* al-Ghafir, 40-41; *Fada'il Ashab al-Nabi*, 5.

[94] Bukhari, *Kafala*, 4.

their personal and communal integrity depended on their active participation in jihad. Furthermore, they understood that a Muslim can secure the protection of God only by supporting His religion: *Believers: if you help (the religion of) God, God will help you and make you strong* (47:7). In other words, Muslims who seek protection from going astray must make struggling in the cause of God their sole goal in life.

To understand how this is done, recall how the Prophet and his Companions conducted themselves. When conditions became unbearable, some Muslims were allowed to migrate to Abyssinia. This migration was a kind of jihad to be carried out at that time. After a second migration, all Muslims who remained or had returned to Makka then emigrated to Madina.

There, the foundations were laid for both the first Islamic city-state and a new kind of jihad, one that had to take existing realities into account. Sometimes the Muslims would run and at other times they would go slowly. In other words, jihad needs its own strategy. The Muslims did not retaliate against their tormenters until God gave them permission to do so by revealing the following verse in Madina:

> Permission (to take up arms) is hereby given to those who are attacked because they have been wronged; and God is able to give them victory. They are those who have been driven from their homes unjustly only because they said: "Our Lord is God." Had it not been for God's repelling some men by means of others, cloisters and churches and oratories and mosques wherein the name of God is often mentioned, would have been pulled down. God helps one who helps His religion. God is Powerful, Mighty (22:39-40).

Having borne persecution of every kind for years, the believers responded with enthusiasm. Only the Hypocrites refused to present themselves when the Prophet summoned the Muslims to fight the Makkans. The Hypocrites either sat idly in their homes or fled the battlefield, for they were slaves to their carnal selves and base desires. By contrast, all sincere Muslims hastened the battlefield whenever they were summoned to fight, for jihad was the means of reaching God and eternity. Therefore, they were as enthusiastic in their response as if they had been invited to Heaven.

Everyone considers death disagreeable, and some of the Companions were no exception. As we read in the Qur'an: *Fighting is ordained for you, though it is hateful unto you. But it may happen that you dislike a thing although it is good for you and it may happen that you love a thing although it is bad for you. God knows; you do not know* (2:216). Such dislike is a natural human characteristic. But the Muslims never actually disobeyed God and His Messenger, and in return God granted them success and victory. These victories gave the believers new strength and energy and, while attractive to the neighboring tribes, caused the Makkans great distress.

The Muslims kept their belief vigorous and active by means of jihad. Those who abandon jihad gradually become hopeless pessimists, for they have deprived themselves of the spirit and stop preaching the truth. Those who persevere in jihad never lose their enthusiasm and always try to increase the scope of their activities. Since every good deed results in a new one, Muslims are never deprived of good: *As for those who strive for us, We guide them to our path. God is with the good* (29:69).

There are as many paths leading to the Straight Path as there are numbers of breaths drawn in creation. Whoever strives for His cause is guided by God to one of these paths, and is thereby saved from going astray. Whoever is so guided lives a balanced life, neither exceeding the limits in their human needs and activities nor in their worship and other religious observances. Such balance is the sign of true guidance.

However great the sacrifices made in fighting unbelievers, they nevertheless all constitute the lesser jihad. This aspect of jihad is *lesser* only when compared to the *greater* jihad. The lesser jihad should never be underrated, for it enables Muslims to acquire the title of *holy warrior of Islam* or the rank of martyr. Such titles open the gates to Paradise and secure God's approval.

The lesser jihad consists of striving to discharge religious obligations as perfectly as possible, whereas the greater jihad requires us to fight against our destructive drives and impulses, such as arrogance, vindictiveness, jealousy, selfishness, self-conceit, and all carnal desires.

Those who abandon the lesser jihad are liable to spiritual deterioration, due to their vulnerability to worldly weaknesses. But they can recover. Pride and love of comfort and ease may captivate Muslim soldiers returning from a victorious battle, for they may think that now it is time to relax and indulge in such things. To fight this tendency, the Prophet warned us through his Companions. Once, when returning to Madina after a victory, he said: "We are returning from the lesser jihad to the greater jihad." [95]

The Companions were as fierce as lions on the battlefield, and as sincere and humble as dervishes in worshipping God. They used to spend most of the night praying to God. Once when night fell during a battle, two of them took turns standing guard. One rested while the other prayed. Becoming aware of the situation, the enemy shot many arrows at him. He was hit and bled profusely, but continued to pray. When he finished,

---

[95] *Kashf al-Khafa'*, 1:424.

he woke his friend, who asked in amazement why he had not woken him sooner. He said: "I was reciting *Surat al-Kahf* and did not wish to interrupt the deep pleasure I found therein." [96]

The Companions went into a trance-like state of ecstasy when in prayer, and would recite the Qur'an as if it were being revealed directly to them. Thus they never felt the pain caused by arrows hitting their bodies. Jihad, in its lesser and greater aspects, found complete expression in them.

The Prophet combined these two aspects of jihad in the most perfect way. He displayed monumental courage on the battlefield. 'Ali, one of the most courageous Muslims, admits that the Companions took shelter behind the Prophet at the most critical moments of the fighting. Once when the Muslim army experienced a reverse and began to scatter in the first phase of the Battle of Hunain, the Prophet urged his horse toward the enemy lines and shouted to his retreating soldiers: "I am a Prophet, I do not lie! I am the grandson of 'Abd al-Muttalib, I do not lie!" [97]

He was just as devoted when it came to worshipping God. He was consumed with love and fear of God in his prayer, and those who saw him felt great tenderness toward him. He frequently fasted successive days. Sometimes he would spend the whole night in prayer, which would cause his feet to swell. Once when 'A'isha thought his persistence in prayer was excessive, she asked him why he exhausted himself so much considering that all his sins had been forgiven. "Shall I not be a slave grateful to God?" was his only reply. [98]

---

[96] Ibn Hanbal, *Musnad*, 3:344, 359.

[97] Bukhari, *Jihad*, 52, 61, 67.

[98] Bukhari, *Tahajjud*, 6.

The Prophet was so courageous that when several Makkans came near enough to discover him and Abu Bakr while they were taking shelter in the cave of Thawr, he simply said: "Don't fear; certainly God is with us." [99] On the other hand, he was so tenderhearted that he wept profusely when reciting or listening to the Qur'an. He once requested Ibn Mas'ud to recite a passage. The latter excused himself, saying he could not recite to the one to whom the Qur'an was being revealed. But the Messenger insisted, saying that he enjoyed listening to someone else recite the Qur'an. Ibn Mas'ud then began to recite the Surat al-Nisa'. When he reached: *But how will it be with them when We bring of every people a witness, and We bring you (O Muhammad) a witness against these?* (4:41), the Prophet asked him to stop because, for fear of God, he could no longer bear it. Ibn Mas'ud narrates the rest of the story: "The Messenger was shedding tears so profusely that I stopped reciting." [100]

The Prophet was as tenderhearted as he was courageous. He asked forgiveness from God at least 70 times a day, and repeatedly urged upon his community the need for asking forgiveness from God.[101]

Those who succeed in the greater jihad are almost certain to succeed in the lesser jihad, but the reverse is not true. 'A'isha narrates: "One night the Messenger asked my permission to perform his supererogatory midnight prayer. I said: 'However much I wish for your company, I wish still more to do what you wish.' Then he performed his ablution

---

[99] This incident occurred during the Prophet's migration from Makka to Madina. Bukhari, *Fada'il al-Sahaba*, 2.

[100] Bukhari, *Fada'il al-Qur'an*, 32, 33, 35.

[101] Bukhari, *Da'wat*, 3.

(*wudu'*) and began to pray. He recited: *In the creation of Heavens and the Earth and (in) the alternation of night and day are tokens (of His sovereignty) for people of understanding* [3:190] over and over again, shedding tears until daybreak." [102]

Sometimes he got up to pray without wakening his wife, since he did not want to disturb her sleep. 'A'isha narrates:

> One night I woke up to find the Messenger was not there. Thinking that he might be visiting another of his wives, I became very jealous. I started to get up, when my hand touched his feet in the darkness. He was prostrating and saying in his prayer: "O God, I seek refuge in Your pleasure from Your wrath, I seek refuge in Your forgiveness from Your punishment. O God, I seek refuge with You from You, I seek refuge in Your grace from Your torment, in Your mercy from Your majesty, and in Your Compassion from Your irresistible power. I am not able to praise You as You praise Yourself." [103]

Being well aware of the obligation to follow his every action, his Companions did their best to be worthy of his company in the Hereafter. Some became physically distressed at the thought of being parted from him in the next life. For example, Thawban lost his appetite after he was unable to participate in a military expedition. On the Prophet's return, everyone went out to meet him. Thawban was so pale that the Messenger asked about his health. Thawban replied:

> O Messenger, I am obsessed with fear of being parted from you in the Hereafter. You are the Messenger, so you will enter Paradise, but I don't know whether I shall deserve it. And even if God admits me, your abode cer-

---

[102] Ibn Kathir, *Tafsir: Al-'Imran*, 190.

[103] Muslim, *Salat,* 22; Haythami, *Majma' al-Zawa'id*, 10, 124; Tirmidhi, *Da'wat,* 81.

tainly will be very much above mine. In this case, I shall
not be able to be in your company forever. I don't know
how I will be able to bear this, seeing that I cannot
endure 3 days' separation from you in this world.

Thawban's worries were relieved when the Messenger
told him: "You will always be in the company of the one
whom you love." [104] To love someone means to follow his or
her example in this life, and the Companions were more
attentive to this than any other people.

'Umar was very eager to establish a family relationship
with the Messenger, for he had heard the latter say that all
genealogical connections would be useless in the Hereafter,
except for those with his own household. Although the Prophet held 'Umar's hand many times and said: "We will be this
(like the two hands together) in the Hereafter too," 'Umar still
desired the family connection. He tried to achieve this by marrying Fatima, but she would only marry 'Ali. He married his
daughter Hafsa to the Prophet and, in the later years of his
caliphate, married 'Ali's daughter Umm Kulthum. If he had
wished, he could have married a neighboring king's daughter.
But he wanted to be allied to the Prophet's household.

Once Hafsa said to 'Umar: "My dear father, from time to
time foreign envoys come and you receive embassies. You
should change your garment for a new one." 'Umar was
shocked by this suggestion and replied: "How can I endure to
part company with my two friends, the Prophet and Abu
Bakr? I must follow their example so strictly that I can be
with them in the Hereafter."

The Messenger and his Companions succeeded in the
greater jihad, and their devotion to God was very strong.

---

[104] Bukhari, *Adab,* 96; Muslim, *Birr,* 1:650.

They spent so much of their time praying that those who saw them thought they did nothing else. But this was not the case, for they led thoroughly balanced lives.

They were very sincere in their deeds, since they did everything for the sake of God and constantly disciplined themselves. Once when 'Umar was giving a sermon, he suddenly said without any apparent reason: "O 'Umar, you were a shepherd pasturing your father's sheep." When asked after the prayer why he had said this, he answered: "It came to my mind that I was the caliph, so I became afraid of feeling proud." One day he was seen carrying a sack upon his back. When asked why he was doing this, he replied: "I felt some pride within me, so I desired to get rid of it." A later caliph, 'Umar Ibn 'Abd al-'Aziz, once wrote a letter to a friend and then tore it up. When asked why, he explained: "I prided myself on its eloquence, so I have torn it up."

Only jihad performed by such perfect souls produces effective results. Those who have not abandoned pride, self-regard, and insincerity most probably will damage the cause of Islam greatly. I would like to emphasize that such people will never obtain the desired result.

Some Qur'anic verses or chapters describe both types of jihad. One of them is: *When the help of God comes, and victory, and you see men entering God's religion in throngs, then glorify the praise of your Lord, and seek His forgiveness; for He is Relenting, Merciful* (110:1-3). When the believers performed the lesser jihad, whether by fighting, preaching, or enjoining right and forbidding wrong, God's help and victory came, and people began to enter Islam in throngs. At that moment, the All-Mighty decreed that His praises should be glorified and His forgiveness sought. As all success and victory is from God, He must be praised and worshipped.

If we can combine our triumph over the enemy with our triumph over our carnal selves, we will have performed jihad completely. 'A'isha narrates that after the revelation of these verses, the Messenger often recited this prayer: "I glorify You with praise, O God. I seek Your forgiveness, and I turn in repentance to You." [105]

The Prophet expresses these two aspects of jihad together in one of his sayings: "The eyes of two persons will never witness Hellfire: the eyes of the soldier who guards the frontier and on the battlefield, and the eyes of those who shed tears for fear of God." [106] The first person is engaged in the lesser jihad; the latter is engaged in the greater jihad. Those who succeed in their jihad will escape the torment of Hell.

We must consider jihad in its entirety. Those who say one thing and then do another cause nothing but trouble in the ranks of Muslims. Since they cannot discipline themselves and overcome self-regard, ostentation, and the desire to dominate, they bring only disharmony to the cause of Islam. On the other hand, those who live in almost total seclusion and try to attain some high spiritual station without working to promote the truth merely reduce Islam to a "spiritual" system, like certain aspects of yoga. Such people argue that a Muslim's foremost duty is to acquire spiritual maturity so as to be saved from Hell. What they fail to realize is that those who regard themselves as safe from Hell are deceived, for God decrees that we should continue to serve Him as long as we live: *And serve your Lord till the inevitable (death) comes unto you* (15:99).

---

[105] Tirmidhi, *Da'wat,* 81.

[106] Tirmidhi, *Fada'il al-Sahaba: Jihad,* 12.

Muslims should never regard themselves as safe from the torments of Hell or give up hope of God's grace and forgiveness. They should tremble with fear of God, as 'Umar did. However, this fear should not prevent them from hoping to enter Paradise: *But for those who fear the standing before their Lord there are two Gardens* (55:46).

In short, jihad consists of self-control and preaching the truth. It requires overcoming one's carnal desires and encouraging others to do the same. Neglecting the former produces social anarchy, while neglecting the latter results in laziness. Today we must achieve a true understanding of Islam in general, and of jihad in particular. This can be realized only through strictly following the Prophet's Sunna.

Are Muslims guilty of imperialism?

This charge continues to be leveled against the Muslim world. I would like to counter it by asking the following questions:

Given the existing circumstances of 1,400 years ago, how would anyone living in Makka or Madina go about exploiting his own clan and tribe? If the supposedly exploited lands and people were those of the Hijaz, which were poor, unfruitful, and barren, who would have wished to invade or exploit them? It is ludicrous to level the charge of imperialist colonialism against the most noble-minded Muslims, who risked their lives to spread the message of Islam; who spent the greater part of their lives far from their children, families, homes, and native lands fighting armies ten or twenty times their size; and who felt deeply grieved when they did not die on the battlefield and join the earlier martyrs for Islam. We ask ourselves what worldly gain they obtained in return for such struggle, deprivation, and sacrifice!

Those who invaded, occupied, and exploited others with the worst intentions (and results) of imperialism are power-hungry individuals or nations. To mention a few: Alexander the "Great" and Napoleon, the Roman empire and Nazi Germany, the Mongol armies unleashed by Genghis Khan and the colonizing armies unleashed by western Europe, Russian dictatorship (whether czarist or communist) and the American empire (whether "manifest destiny" or "making the world safe for democracy"). Wherever such conquests came and went, they corrupted the morality of the conquerors and the conquered, causing chaos, conflict, tears, bloodshed, and devastation. Today their heirs, like bold thieves who bluff property owners to conceal their theft of that very property, turn to besmirching Islam, its Prophet, and his Companions.

True Muslims have never sought to exploit others. Nor have they let others do so where Muslim government had jurisdiction. At a time when Muslim armies were running from triumph to triumph, Caliph 'Umar said: "What befits me is to live at the level of the poorest Muslims," and he really did so. As he took only a few olives a day for his own sustenance, who was he exploiting?

After one battle, when a Muslim was asked to take the belongings of an enemy soldier whom he had fought and killed, he said: "I did not participate in the battle to take spoils." Pointing to his throat, he continued: "What I seek is an arrow here and to fall as a martyr." (His wish was granted.) While burning with the desire for martyrdom, who was he exploiting?

In another battle, a Muslim soldier fought and killed a leading enemy who had killed many Muslims. The Muslim commander saw him pass by his dead enemy. The commander went to the head of the dead soldier and asked who had killed him. The Muslim did not want to reply, but the commander called him back in the name of God. The Muslim felt himself obliged to do so, but concealed his face with a piece of cloth. The following conversation took place:

> - Did you kill him for the sake of God?
> - Yes.
> - All right. But take this 1,000 dinar piece.
> - But I did it for the sake of God!
> - What is your name?
> - What is my name to you? Perhaps you will tell this to everyone and cause me to lose the reward for this in the afterlife.

How could such people exploit others and establish colonies all over the world? To speak frankly, those who hate Islam and Muslims are blind to the historical truth of how Islam spread.

Let's look at what exploitation and imperialism are. Imperialism or colonization is a system of rule by which a rich and a powerful country controls other countries, their trade and policies, to enrich itself and gain more power at the other's expense. There are many kinds of exploitation. In today's world, they may take the following forms:

- Absolute sovereignty by dispossessing indigenous people in order to establish the invader's direct rule and sovereignty. Examples are western Europe's conquest of North and South America, as well as Australia and New Zealand, as well as the Zionists' conquest of Palestine.

- Military occupation so that the invaders can control the conquered nation's land and resources. One example is British colonial rule in India.

- Open or secret interference and intervention in a country's internal and foreign affairs, economy, and defense.

Examples are those Third World countries who are manipulated and controlled by various developed countries.

- The transfer of intellectuals, which is currently the most common and dangerous type of imperialism. Young, intelligent, and gifted people of the countries to be exploited are chosen, given stipends, and educated abroad. There they are introduced to and made members of different groups. When they return to their country, they are given influential administrative and other posts so that they can influence their country's destiny. When native or foreign people linked to exploiters abroad are placed in crucial positions in the state mechanism, the country is conquered from inside. This immensely successful technique has enabled Western imperialists to achieve many of their goals smoothly and without overtly rousing the enmity of the people they wish to subjugate. Today, the Muslim world is caught in this trap and thus continues to suffer exploitation and abuse.

Whatever kind of imperialism they are subjected to, countries suffer a number of consequences:

- Various methods of assimilation alienate people from their own values, culture, and history. As a result, they suffer crises of identity and purpose, do not know their own past, and cannot freely imagine their own future.

- Any enthusiasm, effort, and zeal to support and develop their country is quenched. Industry is rendered dependent upon the (former) imperial masters, science and knowledge are not allowed to become productive and primary, and imitation is established firmly so that freedom of study and new research will gain no foothold.

- People remain in limbo, totally dependent upon foreigners. They are silenced and deluded by such empty phrases as *progress, Westernization, civilization,* and the like.

- All state institutions are penetrated by foreign aid, which is in reality no more than massive financial and cultural debt. Imports, exports, and development are wholly controlled by or conducted according to the exploiter's interests.

- While no effort is spared to keep the masses in poverty, the ruling classes become used to extravagant spending and luxury. The resulting communal dissatisfaction causes people to fight with each other, making them even more vulnerable to outside influence and intervention.

- Mental and spiritual activity is stifled, and so educational institutions tend to copy foreign ways, ideas, and subjects. Industry is reduced to assembling prefabricated parts. The army tends to become a dumping ground for imperialist countries, for its purchases of expensive hardware ensure the continued well-being of the latter's industries.

We wonder if it is really rational to liken the Islamic conquest to imperialism, which brought disastrous consequences wherever it went.

The victory of Muslim armies never caused a great exodus of people from their homes and countries, nor has it prevented people from working by putting chains on their hands and feet. Muslims left the indigenous people free to follow their own way and beliefs, and protected them in exactly the same way it protected Muslims. Muslim governors and rulers were loved and respected for their justice and integrity. Equality, peace, and security were established between different communities.

If it had been otherwise, would the Christians of Damascus have gathered in their church and prayed for a Muslim victory against Christian Byzantium, which was seeking to regain control of the city? If Muslims had not been so respectful of non-Muslims' rights, could they have maintained security for centuries in a state so vast that it took more than 6 months to travel from one end to another?

One cannot help but admire those Muslim rulers and the dynamic energy that made them so, when we compare them to present-day rulers. Despite every modern means of transportation, telecommunications, and military back-up, they cannot maintain peace and security in even a small area of land.

Today, many scholars and intellectuals who realize the value of Islam's dynamics, which brought about Islam's global sovereignty and which will form the basis of our eternal existence in the Hereafter, expressly tell us that Muslims should reconsider and regain them. While conquering lands, the Muslims also were conquering their inhabitants' hearts. They were received with love, respect, and obedience. No people who accepted Islam ever complained that they were culturally prevented or ruined by the arrival of Muslims. The contrast with the reality of Christian Europe's conquests is stark and obvious.

Early Muslims evaluated the potential of knowledge and art in the conquered lands. They prepared and provided every opportunity for local scholars and scientists to pursue their work. Regardless of their religion, Muslims held the people in high regard and honored them in the community. They never did what the descendants of the British colonialists in America did to the American Indians or in Australia to the Aborigines, the French to the Algerians, or the Dutch to the

Indonesians. On the contrary, they treated the conquered people as if they were from their own people and religion, as if they were brothers and sisters.

Caliph 'Umar once told a Coptic Egyptian who had been beaten by a Makkan noble to beat him just as he had been beaten. When 'Umar heard that 'Amr ibn al-'As had hurt the feelings of a native Egyptian, he rebuked him: "Human beings were born free. Why do you enslave them?" As he went to receive the keys to Masjid al-Aqsa, 'Umar visited and talked to priests in different churches in Palestine. Once he was in a church when it was time to pray. The priest repeatedly asked him to pray inside the church, but 'Umar refused, saying: "You may be harassed by other Christians later on because you let me pray in the church." He left the church's premises and prayed outside on the ground.

These are but a few examples to indicate how Muslims were sensitive, tolerant, just, and humane toward other people. Such an attitude of genuine tolerance has not been reached by any other people or society.

Is reincarnation compatible with Islam?

Reincarnation refers to the doctrine that after death the soul moves on to inhabit another body, then dies again and moves on to another body, until there is no longer any reason for it to do so. It is incompatible with Islam.

Belief in some form of reincarnation can be found in almost all societies, whether primitive or sophisticated. Variations exist according to local and regional differences in faith and popular culture. In the most materialistic societies, whose formal culture denies spiritual life, it is almost fashionable in some circles to hold such pseudo-religious beliefs and claim—whether seriously or not—that the spirits of the dead wander about, sometimes assume physical form, and can influence the living until they settle into their new bodies.

One argument for this doctrine's antiquity is the "evidence" found in ancient literature, such as Ovid's (d. 18 CE) colorful extravagances in which "gods" take on human and animal forms, humans assume different shapes, and so on. But these tales do not constitute a doctrine. The doctrine proper has nothing to do with colorful changes of form, but with a belief that an individual soul must pass through every level of creation and every species of life-form, whether animate or inanimate, sentient or non-sentient.

If we reflect upon this, we soon realize that the doctrine is really a strange elaboration on the soul's immortality. In other words, its kernel is that the soul is immortal. That kernel is true; the rest is not. The doctrine also may have arisen from observing similarities in physical and other traits between parents and offspring. Is it reasonable to obscure the logical biological phenomena of heredity and genetics with the illogical doctrine of reincarnation?

This doctrine is said to have emerged in the Nile basin and then spread to other people, such as to India and than back to Greece. There, the eloquence of the classical Greek philosophers rationalized it into a source of consolation and hope for people who, as we all do, longed for eternity. It entered Judaism by way of the Kabbalists, Christianity through Jewish thinkers, and Islam via the ideas of some Sufis—despite the efforts of Muslim theologians to refute it.

Apologists put forward some "evidence." For instance, the Kabbalists mention the transformation of Niobe (mentioned in the Old Testament) into a marble sculpture, and of Prophet Lot's wife into a statue of dust. Others have referred to a literal transformation of Jews into monkeys and pigs.

Another argument explains instinct and intelligence in animals, as well as the splendors of the plant kingdom, as the product of once-human intelligence and vitality. This idea debases humanity and shames its proponents. We all know that there is a program and predetermined destiny for plants and inanimate creation, but it is rather farfetched to trace the harmony and order we see in those kingdoms to formerly human souls. For example, and in reality, plants have a certain plant-life: a direction of growth toward light and moisture. How can this be construed to mean that its life is the result of a formerly human soul that somehow has worked its way down to a lower level of creation?

Despite efforts to corroborate this assertion, no one has ever received a message from a plant confirming that it contains a once-human soul. Nor have we heard any account from someone that he or she was once the soul of a plant or an animal. The media have publicized some accounts of people recollecting so-called past lives and even recounting specific incidents. However, in cases when such claims are not totally absurd, they can be explained as recollections of what has been seen or read and then, knowingly or otherwise, elaborated and transformed. In short, such accounts are no more than ordinary human fictions.

The fact that Niobe and Lot's wife were transformed into sculptures of marble or dust respectively, even if accepted literally, does not prove reincarnation. What we have here is only a physical transformation, not a soul's transmigration.

As for petrified bodies, that is not an arcane phenomenon. Many such corpses have been found, preserved by the absolute dryness of volcanic ashes. Pompeii was destroyed in 79 CE by Vesuvius' sudden volcanic eruption and remained buried for centuries. Recent excavations have revealed numerous Niobe-like petrified bodies. In these ruins, and in the petrified faces and bodies, so busy in their self-indulgent vices and so secure in their arrogance, we can, if we wish, read the signs of Divine wrath and punishment. Perhaps their way of life was solidified in ash and so preserved to warn future generations. To interpret this as evidence of reincarnation is untenable.

Belief in reincarnation in Egypt, India, and Greece developed out of a distorted version of a once-sound belief in the Hereafter and from a longing for the soul's immortality. Neither in Akhenaton's Egypt nor in Pythagoras' Greece did anyone know of such a distorted idea.

To Akhenaton (d. 1362 BC), when one's life ends in this world, a different one starts in heaven. As soon as one dies, the soul sets off on its journey to reach the "Greatest Court" in Heaven. It goes so high that it reaches the presence of Osiris, and hopes to give an account of itself in words like these: "I have come to Your presence as I was free of sins. Throughout my life, I did everything I could that would make devout people pleased. I did not shed blood or steal. Neither did I make mischief or mean any. I did not commit adultery or fornication." Those who can speak so join Osiris' congregation, while those who cannot, whose evil deeds outweigh their good, are hurled into hell and tortured by demons.

Such sound belief also is witnessed in epitaphs relating to Akhenaton's religion:

> What You have done is too much, and our eyes cannot perceive most of them. O One, Only God! No one possesses such might as You have. It is You who have created this universe as You wish, and You alone. It is You who decree the world suitable for human beings, for all animals, whether big or small, whether they walk on the ground or fly in the sky. And it is You alone who sustain

and nourish them. Thanks to You, all beauties come into
existence. All eyes see You by means of those. Verily,
my heart belongs to You (You are in my heart).

The ideas quoted verbatim above were the things that
were believed in as truth in Egypt some 4,000 years ago.

In ancient Greece, the belief in resurrection and the soul's
immortality were quite sound. The great philosopher
Pythagoras (d. c.500 BC) believed that the soul, on leaving the
body, has a life peculiar to itself. In fact, any soul has this
same kind of life even before it quits the Earth. It is commissioned with some responsibilities on Earth. If it commits any
evil, it will be punished, thrown into Hell, and tormented by
demons. In return for the good it does, it will be given high
rank and blessed with a happy life. Allowing for changes that
might have been made in his views over time, we still can see
that there are fundamental similarities with Islam's creed of
resurrection.

Plato's account is not so different either. In his famous
treatise *The Republic*, he says that the soul forgets the material (corporeal) life totally when it leaves the body. Ascending
into an appropriate spiritual realm, one saturated with wisdom and immortality, it is freed from all the scarcity, deficiency, error, fear, and from the passion and love that afflicted it while it lived on Earth. Now that it is free of all evil consequences of human nature, it is blessed with eternal bliss.

In essence, reincarnation is a distorted version of a sound
belief. Every creed, except Islam, has suffered such distortions. For example, the Divinely revealed religion of
Christianity and the exact identity and role of Prophet Jesus
have been distorted. Without the luminous and clarifying verses of the Qur'an and the influence of Islam, Christianity's formal position on this matter may not have been different.

If Christianity teaches the unity of the soul and body, it owes this to the Muslim savants of Andalusia (Muslim Spain). St. Thomas Aquinas (d. 1274) is one of Christianity's most famous philosophers. The greater part of his new ideas and synthesis were adapted from Islamic teachings. He says in his distinguished book that the key concept of humanity is that the soul and body are united in an apt composite.[107] He adds that animal souls develop with animal bodies, but that human souls are created at some time during early development,[108] and therefore rejects the abstract speculations of the Neoplatonist school.

Through similar mistranslations and various distortions, the ancient Egyptian, Indian, and Greek religions became unrecognizable. The doctrine of reincarnation may well be a distortion of an originally sound doctrine of the soul's immortality and return to the Divine Judgment. After reincarnation was inserted into the beliefs of the ancient Egyptians, it became a central theme of songs and legends throughout the Nile region. Elaborated further with the eloquent expressions of Greek philosophers, it became a widespread phenomenon due to the expansion of Greek influence.

Hindus consider matter as the lowest manifestation of Brahma, and consider the convergence of body and soul as demeaning to the soul, a decline into evil. However, death is believed to be salvation, a separation from human defect, a possible chance to achieve an ecstatic union with the truth. Hindus are polytheistic in practice. Their greatest god is Krishna, who is believed to have assumed a human figure in order to eradicate evil.

---

[107] See his *Summa Theologica* (Part I, Question 90, Art. 4).

[108] Ibid., Art. 3.

Their second greatest god is Vishnu, who has descended into this world nine times in different shapes (human, animal, or flower). He is expected to descend for the tenth time. Since they believe that he will come again in the shape of an animal, killing any animal is absolutely prohibited. This is allowed only during war. In addition, most pious and observant Hindus are vegetarians.

According to their most important holy book, the Vedanta, the soul is a fragment of Brahma that cannot get rid of suffering and distress until it returns to its origin. The soul achieves gnosis by isolating itself from the ego and all wickedness pertaining to the ego, and by running toward Brahma just as a river flows toward the sea. When the soul reaches and unites with Brahma, it acquires absolute peace, tranquillity, and stillness, another version of which is found in Buddhism. There is a cessation of active seeking and a passivity of soul in the latter, whereas the soul is dynamic in Hinduism.

Some Jewish sects adopted reincarnation. After refusing belief in Resurrection and Judgment, the Jews, who can be inordinately covetous of life yet remain fascinated by the soul's immortality, could do little else but accept reincarnation. Later on, the Kabbalists transferred it to the Church of Alexandria through certain regional monastic orders. The doctrine had a negligible effect on the manifestation of Islam. Nevertheless, and most unfortunately, it was introduced to Muslims by the Ghulat-i Shi'a (an extremist Shi'a faction).

All those who believe in reincarnation have one characteristic in common: the belief in incarnation. There is a shared failure of intellect to grasp and accept God's Absolute Transcendence. As a result, people believe that the Divine mixes with the human and that the human can (and does) mix

with the Divine. This mistaken idea is all but universal, with
the exception of Islam. The central figure in each distorted
religion is an incarnation or reincarnation: Aten in Atenism,
Brahma in Hinduism, Ezra (Uzair) in Judaism, Jesus in
Christianity, and 'Ali in the Ghulat-i Shi'a faction (considered
by many as outside the fold of Islam). Allegations that some
Sufi writings and sayings support reincarnation are either
plainly malicious or the result of an absurdly literal understanding of their highly symbolic and esoteric discourse.

Throughout history Muslim scholars in every religious
field, certainly among the 90 percent of Sunnis, have rejected reincarnation as totally contrary to the spirit of Islam. The
reason for this stand is simple: The absolute centrality of the
Islamic beliefs that each person lives and dies according to
his or her own destiny, carries his or her own load, will be resurrected individually and called to answer for his or her intentions and actions and their consequences, and that each person will be judged by God according to the same criteria.

We list below the cardinal reasons why Islam rejects reincarnation.

• Belief in Islam requires belief in the Resurrection and
  Judgment, where justice is meted out to each individual
  soul according to what it did while alive. If the individual
  soul passes into different lives, in which form or personality will it be resurrected, commanded to give account,
  and be rewarded or punished?

• This world is created for test and trial so that the soul can
  derive benefit thereby. One focus of the test is belief in the
  Unseen. According to reincarnation, those who live a bad
  life pass into a lower form of life after death. If that is true,
  they will know the consequences of their former life, and
  life as a test loses its meaning. To get around this, its

adherents say that the soul "forgets" its past existence. If that is true, what is the point of a former life?

- If each individual passes through the cycle of birth, death, and rebirth until eternal bliss (enlightenment) is achieved, God's promises of reward and punishment are meaningless. Why would He engage in such meaningless activity?

- The Qur'an and other Divine Books state that sins will be forgiven as a result of sincere repentance. The point of reincarnation is to "work off" one's sins in order to obtain a better rebirth. Is it not more logical to believe in the ability of God to forgive, when and as He wills, rather than to go through this seemingly unending and cumbersome process to achieve, in essence, the same result?

- Long and tiresome cycles of rebirth are contrary to God's mercy, favor, grace, and forgiveness. If He wills, He takes ordinary, worthless, inferior things and turns them into what is purest, best, and beyond price. Infinite indeed are His blessings and munificence.

- Many followers of the Prophets led wicked lives before embracing Islam. Once they converted, however, they reformed themselves within an incredibly short time and became revered models of virtue for later generations. Some of them surpassed previous followers and came to be even more revered. This indicates that, by the favor of God, people can rise easily and quickly to the summit even if they apparently were bound for Hell. It also shows how unnecessary is the doctrine of souls "graduating" to higher levels of being. Indeed, such a doctrine might actually weaken any incentive to moral effort.

- To believe that God, the All-Mighty, has created an individual soul for each person is part of belief in His

Omnipotence. To believe that only a limited number of souls migrate from body to body argues the illogical proposition that the Omnipotent is not Omnipotent. The sheer abundance of life, its infinite variety, its refusal merely to repeat form is everywhere evident. Out of billions of people, we now know how to prove that each one is absolutely unique—no two fingerprints or genetic codes are exactly alike. This fact of individual uniqueness is found in many Qur'anic verses. Given this, why should we assume that the Omnipotent cannot create an infinite number of individual souls and supply them with an infinite number of bodies?

• Why has no one ever come forward and been able to prove, by means of some marks, signs, or evidence that could confirm their "past-life" memories, adventures, and experiences in different forms and bodies? Where is the accumulated knowledge, experience, and culture of those who have lived more than once or have completed their cycle? If this happened in only one out of a million cases, should we not expect a great number of people now living to have extraordinary virtue and competence? Should we not have met a few of them by now? Where are they?

• When somebody reaches a certain measure of physical maturity or age, should we not expect the soul to emerge with all that it has acquired and achieved during its past lives? Should we not expect prodigies? There have been quite a few prodigies in recorded history. All of their special gifts can be explained as a special combination of genetic characteristics occurring in a particular time and place, which is attributable to Divine Grace and Favor, together with the prodigy's efforts to understand this gift in the tradition and context in which it is given.

- No specifically human faculty has ever been found in a non-human entity. But if reincarnation is true, we should expect such discoveries. If a lower form of life is the punishment for particular evil deeds in the previous life, then, presumably, the good in that life also must be carried forward. In other words, some part of the individual's previous life should be retained in the next life. In this case, we would expect the boundaries of particular forms to burst open frequently—with, for example, plants suddenly showing properties associated with animals. Why have we never seen such events?

- If being a human or an animal is the consequence of one's deeds in a former life, which first existed: the human or the animal, the higher or the lower? Believers in reincarnation cannot agree on any form for the first creature, as every generation implies a preceding generation, for how else can the succeeding generation be considered the consequence of the former? If, as some assert, physical life is an evil, why did the whole thing even start? Why did life begin at all? Reasonable answers have not been forthcoming.

Index

D